IN-DEPTH
ACTING
by DEE CANNON

Foreword by Pierce Brosnan

OBERON BOOKS
LONDON

WWW.OBERONBOOKS.COM

First published in 2012 by Oberon Books Ltd
521 Caledonian Road, London N7 9RH
Tel: +44 (0) 20 7607 3637 / Fax: +44 (0) 20 7607 3629
e-mail: info@oberonbooks.com
www.oberonbooks.com

Cover Design and Book Illustrations by James Illman

Printed, bound and converted
by CPI Group (UK) Ltd, Croydon, CR0 4YY.

Visit www.oberonbooks.com to read more about all our books
and to buy them. You will also find features, author interviews and news
of any author events, and you can sign up for e-newsletters so that
you're always first to hear about our new releases.

IN-DEPTH ACTING

To Doreen Cannon

My mother, friend and mentor –
The biggest inspiration in my life.

Contents

FOREWORD

I have been a working actor all my life; for thirty-six years I have been blessed to make a living doing something which I love to do, act. I was trained as an actor at the Drama Centre in London from 1973-76 by Christopher Fettes, Yat Malmgren, and Doreen Cannon, the mother of Dee Cannon, whose book you now have in your possession.

I read from the first page of this wonderful book with a passion and a sense memory of my days as a student there under the direction and tutelage of these great teachers. To this day I still carry with me their words and their teachings, and now you, who wants to go forth into the world of theatre and film, have in your hands the gift of this great book by Dee Cannon. A book that will stand the test of time for any actor in the making, a book of knowledge and hard-earned commitment to the art of acting which will be passed on from generation to generation.

It never gets any easier to make it look effortless and real but, above all else, truthful. You will want to do it all, you must, it is the only way. You have to be fearless, compassionate and full with the humour and grace of who you are in this life, and ready at all times to share it with the world. It is constant work to be an actor, to be present in life and on stage. To deal with the many disappointments and to deal also with the success you will have when it comes your way. You must always move forward to the next challenge. This is a book that will enable you to find your way through those times when you feel lost, adrift and uninspired, it is a book for those of you who are just starting out on your path with a burning passion, and a need that consumes your days and years, and for me, who has come down the road so far and still needs direction.

So go be the actor you want to be, it takes time, be patient and hard-working; read this book, keep it close, find the best people to work with. It's all in the doing, nothing comes from nothing. Be bold.

Pierce Brosnan

I WANT TO ACT

As a child you were very extrovert, always prancing around in front of the mirror, doing dress up, putting on shows with your siblings, performing songs, characters, possibly even speeches. Maybe you put on little shows in front of your parents, maybe even your extended family. Whenever there were family gatherings, birthdays, Easter, Christmas, it was always your cue to perform. How cute, adorable and funny you were. As you got a bit older perhaps you got involved in school plays and then went on to study drama for A level. Maybe you were encouraged to take the LAMDA exams (Graded Examinations in Communication and Performance). Or perhaps you did none of the above but could crack a good joke at parties or do funny imitations or just had a good personality. Your friends and family always told you, 'You would make a good actor, you're so funny, you should act'. Let's face it, all you have to do is turn on the TV and see so many reality stars, singers, comedians, performing up a storm and going into acting – why not you? Why not indeed! Well, it looks so easy, just watch the soaps, I mean all they're doing is acting naturalistically, what's so difficult about that…? Anyone could do that. And then there's the movie industry, how glamorous and well paid. If only that was me up there, that's what I want to do, be an actor.

There's nothing wrong with having aspirations and ambitions. Thousands of young hopefuls do. There are many ways to break into acting and I'm not setting out to quash anyone's hopes and dreams but talent is cheap and I'm afraid it's not enough to rely on talent alone – the profession is far too competitive for that. I am going to tell you about the reality of the industry and the benefits of training. It would be churlish of me to say there was only one route re training and only one methodology re technique. There are many paths one can take and I'm about to set out, from my many years of experience, what I believe is the best way to go about gaining acting skills and why technique is the key to your success as an actor.

I strongly believe that the actors who apply the system correctly are the actors who stand the better chance of nailing their auditions and booking the job. Whether it be for youth theatre, amateur or professional theatre, musical theatre, film or TV, commercials or modeling, I believe you can apply specific methodology to set you apart from other actors who are just relying on their instinct and talent. What's wrong with using your own natural abilities, I hear you say? Nothing, but why rely solely on your charm, charisma and personality? Once you understand that winging it will only get you so far and a little bit of the right skills will get you quite far, then it seems to me, if you want to be a serious actor, there is only one choice - that is to get some acting technique under your belt *now*.

I believe that acting training is not just about learning skills, it is a holistic approach about grooming and preparing yourself – your mind, body and spirit. You should be fine-tuning your observational, listening and concentration skills as well as developing your imagination and allowing yourself to be forever curious. Don't be afraid to ask questions. Be in touch with your feelings and emotions. You should allow yourself to be open and playful – let your inner child remain active throughout your maturity, otherwise there's a danger of becoming too closed, self-conscious, reductive, serious, analytical and cynical, which is not useful for an actor. You should be aware that as you develop, learn and grow as a human being, the richer you become as a person, the richer you will be as an actor.

1. KNOW THY SELF

I think the Jesuit motto is very apt – 'Give me a child until he is seven and I will give you the man.' I do believe that you should have experienced all the main emotions and feelings in life by the time you're seven years old. Happiness, sadness, fear, jealousy, anger, hate, rage, grief, love, hurt and passion – undoubtedly in their raw unfiltered state. Ironic, because as actors it is necessary to be in touch with all of these feelings but often due to life and circumstances many of these emotions get buried and in some cases get buried very deep. It's your responsibility as an actor to be in touch with your emotions and to grow and develop.

Apart from needing to nurture rich feelings and emotions, the main qualities I think an actor should possess and develop in abundance are:

Passion	Playfulness (childlike)
Sensitivity	Concentration
Imagination	Observation
Intuition	Curiosity
Instinct	Humour
Confidence	Versatility
Vulnerability	Compassion
Naivety	Grace
Openness	Honesty

You need to leave your ego at the door if you want to be a good actor. The profession has no patience for egotists, arrogance, defensiveness and aggressiveness.

Before I get onto the benefits of acting training, I will spend some time talking about all the things you can do to supplement your self-development. This can take many forms. You can do this pre-formal training (drama school), in conjunction with training, post-training and with ongoing training throughout your life.

Some of the things that I'm going to suggest might not seem like training at all – you might consider them pure enjoyment, things you do in life anyway. That's my point; if you like to read a certain type of book, maybe you should progress on to reading different genres. If you don't like to read then you should begin. Broaden your horizons, increase your points of reference. You don't have to become an expert but at the very least you should become familiarized with things outside your own social sphere and comfort zone. If you're choosing to go into the arts you should acquaint yourself not just with the actors or films you like but with *all* aspects of the arts. It can't hurt can it?

Here's a list of things to do: hobbies and skills which could be developed for your own pleasure, to broaden your skills or just evolve as an actor. I believe the hardest thing for an actor is to stay inspired in-between acting work. This list might also help stimulate your creative juices that should always be freely flowing whether you're working, 'resting' or just in your own head daydreaming.

A friendly warning: be careful not to get so immersed in street/youth culture that it inhibits you from being versatile. Pop culture is getting more and more defined (this isn't a comment but an observation); talking slang, having strong physical and speech mannerisms, for example over-using the expressions 'like' or 'know what I mean?'. Other bad habits include going up at the end of each sentence, making everything sound like it's a question even if it's not, and having a certain street clothes style, which can be a uniform of conformity. All I can say is be careful not to define yourself in this way if you want to be a versatile actor. Essentially, you want to be castable and in order to be castable you have to be unclouded and adaptable.

Don't set yourself limitations or be afraid of not being good enough – you never know until you take a dip. You might find inspiration can grow and a small talent you have for something can be developed. You might not want to go it alone, that's often the time great collaborations are born. Learn from your mistakes, that's how you can evolve. Be bold, take risks and don't stifle your creativity – fearing what you're scared of won't get you anywhere. I say, 'Feel the fear and do it anyway.'

Take a leaf from American actors, where confidence doesn't mean arrogance. It means there's an inherent belief in yourself. Confidence can be developed and is key to getting ahead. Don't forget, self-belief is very attractive.

THINGS TO DO

☐ **Watch films**
Dramas, Comedy, Romantic Comedy, Sci-Fi, Action, Blockbuster, Independent, International

☐ **Go to the theatre**
Comedy, Serious, Classical, Musicals, Fringe, West End, Repertory

☐ **Take dance classes**
Jazz, Ballet, Modern, Ballroom, Tap, Salsa, Laban, Alexander Technique, Gym, Pilates, Yoga

☐ **Listen to music**
Classical, Jazz, Musicals, Pop, Opera

☐ **Take singing lessons**

☐ **Watch TV**
Mini Series, Drama Series, Documentaries, News (Local and World), Current Affairs, Politics

☐ **Read**
Fiction, Factual, Biographies, Auto-Biographies, Plays (Modern and Classical), Poetry, Reviews, Newspapers, Periodicals

☐ **Write**
Scribble your thoughts, ideas, dreams and then progress onto fiction, poetry, film scripts, plays, reviews, lyrics.

☐ **Draw**
Start by doodling – you can get some good ideas which could lead on to all sorts of wonderful things.
Paint, graphic design, animation.

☐ **Film-making**

☐ **Go to museums**
Art, History, War, Science, Design, Fashion

☐ **Learn to play an instrument**
Piano, guitar, drums, saxophone, trumpet etc.

☐   **Develop new skills and hobbies**
Driving, Horseback Riding, Fencing, Swimming, Walking, Diving, Fishing, Cooking, Sewing, Gardening, Carpentry, Photography, Travel, etc.

I believe you should try to develop your own opinions and taste. Of course these can change but you should try never to sit on the fence. Everything you do and experience in life helps form your opinions, likes and dislikes. I'm not suggesting that you should become overly opinionated; I'm suggesting you should have opinions, ideas and views. The only way you can grow is by gaining life experience. Be open to your surroundings. Traveling is good as this gives you perspective and points of references, which can make you a more diverse and interesting person. If you have ever had a job, fallen in love, experienced a break up, lost someone you loved, this all adds up to your life experience, which at times can make you feel disempowered, at times inspired and ultimately empowered.

I used to think English actors were not able to emotionally connect. I felt frustrated for years, having worked in so many countries abroad and finding that actors there could access their emotions with relative ease. I used to think, well, why can't British actors do that, why won't they open up? I knew that it was a cultural issue and that a huge percentage of British actors were brought up in traditional families where you don't show your emotions; 'don't air your laundry in public', 'stiff upper lip'. You therefore have many generations of actors keeping their emotions very private. Hence the fear of so-called 'Method Acting'. The perception of Method Acting comes from Lee Strasberg and his Acting Studio doing a lot of sensory exercises, with feelings and emotions at the heart of the training. My take on this is, whereas there is a place for **sense memory**, **affective** and **emotional memory**, I do feel this is homework you do when you need to connect to a feeling or emotion you can't access. *I do not* agree with making this the heart of the training.

If you go back to the time of the legendary Group Theatre in NYC in 1931, which was made up of a body of the new generation of up-and-coming American actors, writers and directors such as Stella Adler, Lee Strasberg, Clifford Odets, Harold Clurman, Cheryl Crawford, Elia Kazan, Robert Lewis and Sanford Meisner to name but a few. They were looking for another style of acting and they heard about this actor Konstantin Stanislavski in Russia who had founded a fresh methodology. The story goes that Stella Adler went over to Russia to meet Stanislavski and find out about this new 'System' of acting. She brought it back to 'The Group' and they were all very excited about finding this fresh, truthful and real way of acting as opposed to the 'Old School' way which was over the top and external – 'Melodrama.'

There were new writers and playwrights coming out of Russia who were desperate for novels and theatre to reflect 'Realism' and psychological subtext; writers such as Turgenev, Gogol, Gorky, Chekhov, Tolstoy, Pushkin and Bulgakov. The Moscow Arts Theatre needed a new style of acting which would suit 'Realism'. Stanislavki's system worked and changed the face of Russian theatre; Moscow Arts Theatre in particular became the face of 'Socialist Realism' in Russia and 'Psychological Realism' in the USA.

After awhile the Group Theatre got a little bit confused and stuck in a rut with the new 'system', which at this time was based primarily around **sense memory, emotional memory** and **affective memory**. They needed something more. Stella Adler went back to visit Stanislavski and told him of their difficulties and he said that he doesn't use 'memory' as the chief principle of acting anymore; he had come up with his latter work, **physical action**. This was based on physical and psychological 'action'. Adler returned satisfied that this was the missing link. The Group Theatre agreed, this was the ingredient they needed, except for Lee Strasberg who was convinced that **memory recall** was the key to unlocking an actor and was the foundation of 'truthful acting'. He quit, turned his back on 'The Group' and started his own 'Actors Studio' and the metamorphosis of Method Acting evolved. To this day Method Acting is synonymous with Strasberg, even though Stella Adler and Sanford Meisner, and subsequently Uta Hagen and Herbert Berghof went on to teach and form their own studios; all believed in Stanislavki's **action** work as the primary source of the training alongside 'imagination' and Stanislavski's the 'magic if.'

I can't say Lee Strasberg's approach is particularly healthy. He encouraged introspection and saw himself as a therapist, convinced that real emotion sprang from an actor's personal history. Unfortunately, Method Acting is almost solely associated with emotional and sensory memory; revealing and reliving emotional traumas in order to bring you closer to yourself and your feelings and therefore closer to your character; submerging yourself totally into your character by actually living and breathing them twenty-four hours a day.

I'm unconvinced that by neglecting 'action' and 'imaginative' work you become more connected to the character. In my honest opinion, I think this promotes emotional, self-absorbed, indulgent and boring actors that have no regard for audiences; performances (mainly on stage) being mumbled in an effort to be truthful and naturalistic, or shouted to show so-called emotion. I'm sad to say this has not helped the credibility of Method Acting in the UK as its perception is scary, self-indulgent and at its worst psychotherapy. I don't call what I teach 'Method Acting'; there are too many negative connotations. I much prefer to call it 'Acting Technique' based on Stanislavski's teachings.

Famous Method actors include James Dean, Marlon Brando, Montgomery Clift, Marilyn Monroe, Anne Bancroft, Dustin Hoffman, Julie Harris, Al Pacino, Robert De Niro and Paul Newman. However, contrary to popular belief, only a few of these actors trained exclusively with Lee Strasberg and many, many other actors floated between Stella Adler, Uta Hagen, Herbert Berghof, Mira Rostova and Sanford Meisner.

Let's return to my earlier point about British actors not being emotionally connected. I believe that in the last five years there has been a noticeable change and I now feel actors are connecting more and more to their emotions. In a strange way, I think this is due to the surge of reality TV shows, where it's commonplace for judges and contestants to wear their heart on their sleeves. I'm not saying this in a negative light at all, on the contrary, the fact that we see a plethora of judges, contestants and audiences alike on shows like *X Factor, Britain's Got Talent* and *American Idol* openly crying and showing their emotions, it's clear, it no longer seems taboo to show your feelings.

I think this acceptance of emotion spills over into daily life with family and friends. Whereas before feelings might have been repressed, now, expressing your emotions seems decidedly less self-conscious and far more tactile – openly hugging, kissing and crying has now become the touchstone of normality. I'm happy to say, in my training of young British actors I have recently noticed more willingness to show emotion, vulnerability and less reticence, covering up and burying feelings. There seems to be more of an acceptance that you have to be less private and dig a bit deeper if you want to be an actor with some depth. I think the old British adage of 'stiff upper lip' and 'men don't cry' is way out of date and is a throw back to the pre- and post-war generation. British society has become a melting pot of different cultures and this is slowly filtering into UK society, opening up an emotional spectrum, which is of course very healthy.

I strongly believe as an actor, you should be working on yourself all the time. Developing your skills, cultivating yourself and understanding what makes you tick. For example, what makes you happy, sad, angry, upset, laugh, melancholic, jealous, bitter, immature, childlike, insecure, aggressive, feminine, macho? You should over time not only be able to answer these questions but be able to access these feelings and emotions when needed. As an actor you should have access to all areas. I believe you have to emotionally connect to your feelings, you must have fire in your belly, not only in your everyday life but also as an actor. If your emotions are blocked in any way or are off-kilter you need to recognize that as an actor you need to be self-aware and start to develop your emotions or in some circumstances lessen your emotional availability. In some instances this might mean making certain adjustments or just allowing yourself to be more expressive. In other cases you might have developed blocks which could subside over time or if the blocks are very deep-rooted you might have to seek professional help in order to unblock yourself.

I would say, if you weren't going into the acting profession it shouldn't matter if you were in touch with yourself or not, nor if you are emotionally stifled. If your intention is only to be a representational actor and you don't see the connection between finding your own emotional depth and showing it in your character, then ignore the above. However, if you do want to be an actor who shows great depth in your characters then I can't stress enough how crucial it is to find the emotional depth within yourself. As I said before, the more you can develop, learn and grow as a human being, the richer you become as a person, the richer you will be and grow as an actor. This is what I think every actor should be striving to achieve. In CHAPTER 6(i) I outline certain exercises I do which can bring hidden feelings and emotions to the surface and with careful orchestration this can be a freeing, releasing and hugely cathartic experience.

2. WHY TRAIN?

You have the talent and someone in your family knows someone who knows this agent who might agree to meet with you. If you get signed, you might get a chance to be in a feature film, a soap or a TV series. Maybe it's your own initiative that secures you an agent – you have the right look and get a few small parts that land you a big part. I know from experience this can happen quite successfully and I have worked with many, many actors, models and singers who have got their lucky break without any formal training behind them. However, it's no coincidence they have come through my door for private coaching. They all have something in common; they have realized that their talent, instinct and good fortune has only got them so far but they have reached a road/career block which can't take them any further. This block is lack of resource, technique; their natural abilities have taken them thus far but they just don't have the knowledge or skills to take them to the next level.

Let's take the analogy of a painter and decorator grafting. If you needed your house or apartment painted, you would never hire someone to come and just put on the final coat of gloss paint would you? You would expect all the prep work to be done first, otherwise the final gloss of paint will go on uneven, bumpy and perhaps start to bubble or peel. They clean the walls, rub them down with sandpaper, fill in the holes with Polyfilla, put on an undercoat/primer and then another coat before the final coat, the gloss paint, finally gets applied.

As an actor, dancer or singer how could you possibly think of getting up and performing without putting in the time to prep and train. Dancers and singers would never dream of going on stage without their warm up and preparation so why should an actor. You have to graft your trade. Your voice, body and mind are muscles and without the essential core skills you can never expect to have a career in the industry.

Let me break this down for you a bit more. Often for film and TV you are cast to type, unlike theatre which is more challenging and where you can often be cast older or younger than your years – your casting can be quite transformational and stretching on stage. This happens a lot less on film and TV. If you're the right type and have the right look you might well be cast in a film, soap or TV series that requires you to play very close to yourself and your own age. You could have great success in your running part or even get to do as many as eight feature films playing variations of yourself. The problem comes when the film or soap ends and you're feeling very confident and you go up for another role that you're not naturally ready-made for, that requires using another side of yourself. Perhaps you need to be vulnerable, stronger, manipulative...? You find this hard to achieve and don't do well in your audition or the next one and soon your confidence starts to wilt and eventually drops to an all-time low. So what happens now? How do you access a different side of yourself when you've just been using one aspect that has kept you in work for quite awhile...?

Another very common scenario I hear from soap/film actors who haven't trained, arises when they're asked to do a very emotionally loaded scene and have to break down and cry. They've worked themselves up on the way to the studio, in their trailer and consequently they're able to find the emotion in their first take – *bravo*! This is all because their focus has been on being able to cry on cue. The director is delighted and everyone's happy, which just goes to prove, if you think about sad moments in your life for long enough it can work. Ah, but what happens when they need to do another take...? The light wasn't quite right, the sound was muffled, the other actor forgot his lines... Yikes, you have to do it all over again, but this time you don't have three hours to psych yourself up. Everybody's waiting and you have to reproduce the emotion you found twenty minutes ago... OK maybe you're still feeling vulnerable and you squeeze out a few more tears for the second take but nowhere near as good as the first. What about after the sixth? What if this scene comes right before the lunch break and there's no time to go back to your trailer to get back in the mood, everyone around you is talking and you sense an impatience, all everybody wants to do is break for lunch... Your tears dry up and there's no way you can get back the feeling you had for your first take in the morning. You get tense and angry at yourself, which isn't helping and is throwing your performance, and perhaps you also forget your lines and the director is polite but fuming inside that the actor he hired cannot sustain emotion. This kind of scenario tends to happen when you're relying on your natural instinct and a good conducive environment. It doesn't help if you're not sure how you got from A to B and only pray you can get to that point again... This is exactly why you need technique. If you know how to get there, you can do it again and again and again!

Still not convinced? Let me reverse this scenario. What about the night before your first big day of filming for your first major film part, you receive some devastating news on the phone. It has shattered you and you have been up all night crying. Or maybe you've just found out your girlfriend or boyfriend has been cheating on you and you have a massive argument which culminates in one of you walking out and you don't get any sleep and your eyes are red and sore from crying all night. Your first day of filming is a happy celebration as it's your engagement party or maybe it's your wedding day. How do you pick yourself up from feeling so low and depressed? Where are all your natural instincts today? Deeply buried under a wad of emotions? How do you get them to resurface? You've always relied on them up until now... If only you had some sort of technique that you could fall back on, but you don't, so you muddle through probably the hardest and possibly the least rewarding filming you've ever had to do.

Without acting skills, there are a variety of scenarios that can happen: What happens when you're performing opposite someone you consider dreadful? What if your director isn't good and doesn't direct you or critique you constructively, then what? What happens when you wake up feeling unwell, with a splitting headache/migraine or stomach cramp but still have to rehearse? What happens when nerves kick in and everything you rehearsed at home goes out the window? It's very hard to pull a performance out of the bag, wing it or sustain it if you don't feel well, have a good director or know what you're doing. A trained actor should be able to rehearse feeling unwell or with a lousy director because they should be relying on technique to get them through.

I find the difference between someone who's trained and someone who hasn't usually rears its head in a rehearsal room. There's nothing more frustrating for me than spending a whole day rehearsing a few scenes, detailing, blocking and solving character problems and finding the next time we rehearse these scenes that nothing has been retained and I find myself back to square one with the actors. This rarely happens with a trained professional who can usually sustain direction and I find that when I work with them again the scene and their performance go to the next level; this leads to growth, breadth and depth.

So does training rob you of your natural instincts? On the contrary, I strongly believe that training enhances your natural instincts and backed up with technique makes you a fully rounded and equipped actor.

Training will ultimately make you much more hirable and should leave you with confidence and discipline under your belt. Talent is cheap, there's plenty of talent out there, but the bright, canny and realistic actors understand you have to invest in training in order to have a sustained career. Whatever path you decide to take I will now endeavor to discuss the different options of training available.

3. ACTING TRAINING

DRAMA SCHOOL

Going to drama school in the UK is the most conventional, formal and expected way to train. The three-year BA courses are the most respected and the most fully rounded training you will receive.

THE ADVANTAGES OF A 3-YEAR TRAINING

Training in acting, voice, movement, text, improvisation, singing, fencing, classical dance, sight reading, overview of history of theatre, classical plays etc.

Three years of drama school training can give you longevity in the profession. It can also give you confidence, skills and a network associated with that specific drama school. In your last year you are showcased in front of the public, agents and casting directors. Drama school is what you make it. You shouldn't think that just because you've got into a top drama school you can coast or rely on the talents of your teachers and classmates to get you through. I've seen this happen many, many times. After the initial euphoria of getting in and the excitement and nerves of being in a new school with newfound classmates wear off, your hard work ethic should kick in. I have seen many a student leave after three years the same person they came in, as opposed to a developed and transformed young actor and individual.

I was often surprised that students in their final year, who had the privilege to be directed by outside directors (each with their own particular approach), would sometimes have an unfulfilled experience because they expected to be guided and nurtured. The shock of just being directed wasn't what they were used to and was often a big wake-up call. This is of course very healthy and is representative of what they'll find once they leave drama school and go out into professional theatre.

Often I was disappointed by their performances and would frequently enquire as to why they were so untruthful or, in most cases, they would pre-empt my reaction and be only too keen to tell me why I wouldn't like something or think their performance was any good. I would always ask why and they would always say that the director was very external, or encouraged them to be caricature or larger than life, or 'didn't believe in all that Method stuff' and was more interested in the staging and blocking of the play. Fair enough, but why then wouldn't you use the 'work', the technique that you were taught? This is surely why you came to drama school, to be able to find the truth, flesh out your character and find the justifications you need to make sense of your direction. I don't think the excuse that your director doesn't work in the same way as you (or what you believe in) is reason enough. As far as I'm concerned, that is even more grounds for you to put in the work that's needed to make a believable character.

I found that the students who understood this and applied the work regardless, always shone in a mediocre production. It's hard not to be reliant but that is exactly what technique should give you – self-reliance no matter if you have a good director, who can only make your performance more brilliant, or a bad director where it boils down to you to make your performance better. If you use your training correctly you should soak up as many skills as possible and use the three years to make mistakes and ultimately perfect your craft.

As with anything, the more you put in, the more you will get out. Of course you will always find teachers, skills, classmates that you don't understand or get on with. You shouldn't let this hinder your self-development and training. This will inevitably be the case in any institution or workplace. The best advice I can give you is to go with an open mind and soak up as much as you can and put on a top shelf anything you don't like or understand. That way you're not dismissing it completely and you can always bring it down at a later date if and when you need to.

Aside from the 3-year BA courses there's an array of 1- and 2-year courses that have popped up. I don't think the training is as thorough but nonetheless it definitely should be considered as a supplement to further training. Three years is better than two and two is better than one – one is better than no training.

MAs Up until a few years ago an MA was something you did if you wanted to go into teaching, writing or directing. Now you can take an MA in almost every aspect of theatre including acting. Taking an MA in Acting has really grown in popularity in the last few years; it's geared for the slightly older student and should definitely not be sniffed at. You have to realize of course that you won't be covering acting in quite as much depth as a BA due to the fact that MAs are usually only a year long.

MFAs are two-year courses and you will definitely get more performance experience if you opt for a second year.

WORKSHOPS

You can find a plethora of workshops varying from good, mediocre to poor. You should never view a workshop as a complete training. Workshops are usually topping up your skills. Workshops for beginners usually serve as an overview and are a valuable step to take as a novice. I would encourage you to take various workshops to expose yourself to different teachers and work with other people.

In NYC and LA there are very few formal drama programmes and the majority of actors spend their careers dipping in and out of various workshops and classes.

We don't really have weekly acting classes in the UK although we do have this set-up with dance lessons.

FILM ACTING COURSES

These courses are not a substitute for learning to act or a back door into the film-acting profession. Although I think certain film courses serve a purpose, you should be careful about spending lots of money because these courses are easier to get into than drama school. In reality there's no such thing as film acting – acting is acting and you need to know who your character is whether it's for stage or screen. As far as I'm concerned, there's an adjustment that has to be made when acting in front of a camera as opposed to acting on stage. The obvious being that on stage you have to train your voice and body because you have to articulate and make sure the audience can hear you. In film you don't have to worry about your voice as much; you are wired up so the sound can pick up every breath you take. Therefore, for film you have to be connected and as on point as you can re your character, because, the camera will pick up every nuance, gesture, reaction you make. On screen there's no need to be over-animated – the less you do/show the better.

Which brings me back to why spend money on a film course as opposed to an acting course. Yes, you need to find your mark and know certain technical aspects but that's what a screen acting course should do, serve the purpose of gaining experience in front of a camera before you actually work in front of a camera. It's easier to make mistakes in a workshop rather than on a job. Therefore I suggest if you have a burning desire to do one of these courses, make sure you have some acting training behind you to make the most of what the course has to offer.

PRIVATE COACHING

I have seen an increase in beginners and professionals wanting one-to-one coaching. This can serve as a good way to gain confidence and skills in a private and personal environment. I often think the best use of a coach is in conjunction with workshops or alongside an acting job.

I understand why young actors seek private coaching to get into drama school. After all gaining a place is very competitive and I find myself guiding, mentoring and helping them make the right choices so that they stand a good chance of being accepted on to a course.

The advantage of seeking private coaching is that you can bespoke your training to exactly what you need. Not everyone gains a place at drama school and sometimes it's not the right path for someone older or someone who has a fair amount of acting experience under their belt. Private coaching can also act as a springboard for actors who trained years ago and are now in need of a refresher to be able to re-enter the profession. Equally, this is the case with latecomers who have decided after a few years, or in some cases many years, in another profession not to go through the route of drama school due to time and age but who still want a shot at a career. Formal training doesn't suit everyone and it's no longer the case you *have* to go to drama school to get good training. You could take the large amount of money you would pay for one year at a drama school and put it towards finding the best Acting coach, Voice teacher, Singing teacher, Alexander teacher and you will virtually have your own tailor-made training at your own pace and with personal individual attention you might not receive elsewhere.

A lot of my coaching also tends to be with celebrities who don't want to put themselves in a class situation; they want the privacy, convenience and trust of their coach.

Whatever route you decide to take, I hope you will gain enough tools and skills to prepare you for this precarious but wonderful profession.

4. AUDITIONS

Auditioning is a fairly contrived process because you have to learn a monologue that has been taken out of context from a play. Obviously in its natural setting on stage you're talking to another character but when you're auditioning you have to cut out the other character and talk to thin air or an empty chair as if there's someone there. However, even though this process might seem artificial to you, it's quite a good way for the people auditioning you to see if you can emotionally and textually connect to the material you have chosen – in other words to see if you can *act*!

There's no point complaining about how unfair the audition system is: 'If only I wasn't so nervous', 'How can they tell from only two pieces?', 'I did it much better at home the day before', ' I felt I chose the wrong pieces', 'I really messed up', 'I could tell they didn't like me'. I hear you moan. All I can say is get over it.

If you want to have a career in this profession, you need to learn the art of 'How to audition'. This is key to gaining a place to train, which in turn will allow you your first entry into the profession once you graduate. Of course this doesn't mean your audition days are over, in fact they've only just begun but at least if you earn a place at drama school you won't have to worry about auditioning for a few years.

I feel there is an art to auditioning and that it's worth trying to learn and refine it so that you can have a long and successful career. Granted, you can give a really good audition and still not gain a place or get that role due to factors outside your control – too young, too old, too tall, too small. I can't help you there but I can help you try to nail your audition technique.

DRAMA SCHOOL AUDITIONS

The biggest misunderstanding about preparing for your audition is to choose monologues/characters that you have always aspired to perform. Nine times out of ten these are the wrong choices for you! There's no point trying to be ambitious and challenging yourself with a speech that is way out of your league and age range. For example, here are some characters that if you're between 18–25 and you're auditioning to drama school you should avoid: Macbeth from *Macbeth*, King Lear from *King Lear*, Richard III from *Richard III*, Stanley Kowalski from *A Streetcar Named Desire*, Blanche DuBois from *A Streetcar Named Desire*, Martha from *Who's Afraid of Virginia Woolf?*, Lady Macbeth from *Macbeth*, Queen Margaret from *Richard III*.

Why? Why do that to yourself? As far as I'm concerned, you're setting yourself up to fail! OK, so maybe you will do it brilliantly – great! You will be the exception. It takes guts, talent and confidence to pull it off. It's risky and although I have seen it done with great aplomb, which in itself is to be applauded, it's a gamble I don't encourage. I believe you should pick characters within your age range. They don't have to be your exact age, there's no reason why you can't go up a few years or down a few years but try to choose something that is believable casting.

I recently had a young guy come to me, wanting help on his audition pieces. He had chosen a black American, drug addict, Jazz musician. He was neither black, American, a drug addict (past or present) or indeed a jazz musician or a musician in any way. He just liked the speech, it was cool. Needless to say I convinced him to find something closer to home and he felt much more comfortable and connected once we found something that he could bring a truthful reality to.

I think you should try and typecast yourself when it comes to looking for the most suitable audition pieces. It makes sense if you think about it. Why would you show them what you *can't* do, as opposed to what you *can* do? You don't want them to see you struggle to connect with a character who's married and divorced with three kids when you're barely out of school. Does that mean you're confined to playing young students? Not necessarily, but young, yes. You can find young parents or professionals but the key here is being able to emotionally engage with what you choose, otherwise don't choose it. You're never going to find a speech that fits you exactly and that's what your stretch is going to be – finding the truth of a character that's outside of you. Isn't that hard enough? You therefore shouldn't be choosing anything too far away!

Be careful not to be seduced by a well-written, juicy role that you yearn to play one day and that you might've seen performed by an extremely talented actor. All I'm suggesting is, you can still yearn but be realistic in your choices. I can spend hours with young students trying to help them find something. I can pass them on pieces that I think are suitable but if they don't connect with what the character is going through then there's no point choosing the piece. It's worth taking some time to scour audition books or plays to find something you like and that is appropriate. It must be something you like though; if you find something that is suitable but you don't respond to it, don't choose it. It can be tiring and daunting but I can assure you, if you persevere, you will find the right monologues.

Always dress appropriately for your audition i.e. wear something quite neutral in colour and attire. It can be very off-putting for the panel to watch you perform for example Shakespeare in shorts, torn jeans and loud T-shirts with inappropriate logos and images.

ACCENTS AND DIALECTS

This is something that comes up all the time. Should I do an accent, or should I not do an accent? I will talk from common sense here. Why choose a piece in which your character is from Ireland/Scotland/Wales/Manchester/Yorkshire and requires a dialect if you're from London and are not very good at doing dialects? Don't choose it! However, if you are from a different country or region, or from even further afield – America, Brazil, South Africa, Italy, Spain or France – finding a good play that's translated and that's set in your part of the world would be quite canny. Not only would it suit your accent but there's a good chance you will be able to relate to the material much more than if it were set in East London and you've only just moved here a few months ago. Good writers are not just from the UK or America but from all over the world so if you are, say, from Sweden/Spain/Germany please look to your own gifted writers first and foremost and then try to find a good translation of the plays that you like. I'm sure this will not only suit your temperament, rhythm and cultural style but it will also be hugely refreshing, interesting and original for the audition panel, not to mention a talking point.

NCI7443

There are a few drama schools that don't encourage accents other than your own to be used and this is because there's nothing worse than someone doing a monologue with an exaggerated, over-the-top, generalized accent that dominates the whole speech. This is something to avoid, but if you have chosen a well-known monologue from famous American writers like Arthur Miller, Tennessee Williams, Neil Simon or Beth Henley, then I think it would be whole-heartedly wrong to use your own accent, unless of course you're American. This is because these are prominent playwrights who have written very specifically about these characters growing up in their particular town, with their own dialects, idioms, cultural and political references. If the references were particularly apposite to American society (for example Thanksgiving, Vietnam, Korean wars, cheerleading, baseball) it wouldn't make sense in the context of the speech if you had a very strong South London accent. If you have chosen something widely known and specific to American culture, I would use an American accent as long as it doesn't detract from the speech itself.

I think it's absolutely fine to have a generalized American accent. It doesn't have to be perfect and you shouldn't be stressing about the accent or seeking help to try to perfect it. It should blend in with the speech and should not take over so that all you hear or notice is the accent. If you are meant to have a Southern accent then you should attempt one, the rhythm is markedly different from someone from the East or West coast.

If you're not confident with accents or dialects you should stay away from speeches where you'll need to have one. If, on the other hand, you really connect with the speech and the character is, say, from Germany and you really want to attempt the accent, find some key German phrases and perfect those; that should help you every time you want to transition into the accent or dialect of the speech.

CLASSICAL MONOLOGUES

It is without question more daunting to find and relate to a classical monologue than a modern one. Nonetheless, you still have to find one or two contrasting pieces to get into drama school. Where do you start? Sometimes it helps to refer back to plays that you have already studied or been in, in school. This of course wouldn't necessarily serve you if you didn't have a good experience or like the play or if you felt the selection of monologues wouldn't work taken out of context of your school production.

Realistically speaking you can't really be that original with a classical speech as there are only a handful that are age appropriate and you can be sure that other applicants will also be choosing them. That said, you can focus on making a clever choice and work hard to make sense of what you're doing and saying. There are several pitfalls that you should avoid:

☐ Read the play you're thinking of doing a monologue from. This might seem obvious to you but you will be surprised by the amount of young students who choose their speeches off the internet and it's either not occurred to them to read the play or they're just too lazy. Personally, I won't work with anyone who can't be bothered to put in the work. If you haven't got much time and you're panicking that you're auditioning at the last minute, reading the play is essential! If it's the only thing you do, read the play, otherwise how can you make sense of what you're saying? You need the context. And I don't think it's acceptable that you go online and only look at the synopsis; that is not a substitute. I also don't accept the excuse that Shakespeare is too hard and scary. If that's the case, even more reason to read the play and try to understand it. I highly recommend buying Shakespeare study notes to guide you while working through the text.

It also can't hurt to try to see a production of the play you're thinking of doing a speech from. If you're really struggling and there's no production currently in the theatre, then try to source the film version. I don't advocate this as a shortcut but I do suggest it if you're having a hard time understanding the text. Especially if English is not your first language, watching the film version can be very useful. I wouldn't watch it over and over again and try to study the actor saying your speech or try to imitate how it's said. It might seem tempting but I assure you this will be detrimental to your process and it will be acutely obvious to whoever you're auditioning for that this is an imitation. Treat the film as an aid in helping your understanding of Shakespeare.

☐ You should recognise that you will have to bring the right level of truth to the text and by that I mean you have to find a formal truth (15th/16th Century) because if you bring your own contemporary reality to the speeches it just won't work or make sense. I will talk further about finding the right truth in CHAPTER 5.

☐ Iambic pentameter is the meter that Shakespeare nearly always used when writing in verse – it is the beat of the 16th Century – and it doesn't apply to his prose. I won't be elaborating on this subject, as you will be able to find quite a lot of wonderful books/ online resources dealing with this topic. What I will point out, is that you must adhere to Shakespeare's text. You must not ad lib or add your own punctuation. You must follow the meter as he is guiding you through it.

The most helpful example I can give you is not to break up thoughts or sentences. He tells you when to breathe and you will be able to see this in the punctuation. You will often find long thoughts and if you break the thought up by putting in a pause or because you need to breathe, this can jar the whole meaning of what you are saying. In this instance you will have to work out where you can snatch a breath if the thought/sentence is very long. This is why Shakespeare is considered quite tricky to do; it will show your shortcomings very quickly. Ideally you have to take in enough breath to say the lines. You must then be able to support your breath to be able to sustain your thought all on one breath if need be. In Shakespeare, the thought or feeling is on the line, therefore you have to be able to take the meaning of your thought right through to the end of the sentence.

Unlike contemporary text, there's no subtext in Shakespeare, meaning you can't pause in-between your thoughts (as you would in a modern play) to show that you're angry or unhappy etc. Once you realise this, it might help you recognise the value of the word and help make the language a valuable tool for expressing yourself as the character. No mumbling allowed.

Never negate the text. Never get into the bad habit of paraphrasing the text. Although this applies to Shakespeare and classical text, I do strongly believe this is true of all modern scripts in theatre, film and TV. The words have to be respected alongside subtext and characterization. You should see the words as your tool for communication but if you rely on them alone you have something empty and external.

A good way of trying to make sense of Shakespeare is to contemporise/modernise what you are saying. I get my students to rewrite their speech in their own words – mirroring the **action** and **objectives** of the text.

Edmund from *King Lear* Act I Scene 2

Thou, Nature, art my goddess; to thy law
My services are bound. Wherefore should I
Stand in the plague of custom, and permit
The curiosity of nations to deprive me,
For that I am some twelve or fourteen moonshines
Lag of a brother? Why bastard? wherefore base?
When my dimensions are as well compact,
My mind as generous, and my shape as true
As honest madam's issue? Why brand they us
With base? with baseness? bastardy? base, base?
Who, in the lusty stealth of Nature, take
More composition and fierce quality
Than doth, within a dull, stale, tiréd bed,
Go to th' creating a whole tribe of fops
Got 'tween a sleep and wake? Well then,
Legitimate Edgar, I must have your land.
Our father's love is to the bastard Edmund
As to th' legitimate. Fine word, 'legitimate'!
Well, my legitimate, if this letter speed,
And my invention thrive, Edmund the base
Shall top th' legitimate. I grow, I prosper.
Now, gods, stand up for bastards!

Here is a recent version of one of my private students who, I think, wrote a particularly good interpretation transposing it to someone in his family:

It doesn't matter how I was born.

We all have rights.

And I know it's somewhat normal for you to get everything you want as you are mummy's little boy, who am I to stop routine?

But I am as clever as you, confident as you, even nicer than you.

But why should you get everything?

Don't I deserve it too?

Am I not as good as you?

We both have the same parents don't we?

Aren't we equals?

Fine if you want it this way then you'll have to fight me for it.

Mam' loves me just as much as you.

Once I tell her some home truths, she'll realise what you really are.

I'll make sure you learn what it's like to have nothing.

You'll loose everything you've got and mam' won't be there to pick you up off the floor.

You self-centred, obnoxious little shit.

Fuck you and when I have everything; all the money, a house, all the fucking holidays I want, then I'll come and rub it in your face.

I'll be the bee's fucking knees for a change.

Let's see how rosy life is then.

You'll see, things are going to change.

Things are definitely going to change!

I then got my student to rehearse his own version, until he got all the right **beats/units** (CHAPTER 6(v)), passion and venom behind what he was saying. This was quite an easy process for him, as his speech was personal and heartfelt, therefore the transition into Shakespeare was much easier, more truthful and connected.

Shakespeare Vs Jacobean and Restoration

Many of the drama schools allow you to choose between Shakespeare, Jacobean and Restoration monologues. I often have students who want to choose an alternative to Shakespeare due to the scary nature of the language. To this I would say, think again. Only in some instances I have found Jacobean and Restoration texts to be more accessible.

Elizabethan plays 1558 – 1603 Comedy, History and Tragedy. Shakespeare tends to write about more universal themes: the power of love, loss, magic, dreams, fractious love, misunderstanding, jealousy, ambition and revenge.

Jacobean plays 1603 – 1625 Dark plots filled with horror, blood and violence. Themes often revolve around ambition, corruption, lust, revenge, money, sex, adultery and incest.

Restoration Comedies 1668 – 1710 Comedy of Manners, which reads like a social commentary of the day: wit, urbanity, sophistication, love, sexual intrigue and cuckoldry is at the heart of these plays.

The language of Jacobean and Restoration plays might be less daunting but the themes tend to be harder to connect to. My advice to you would be to read a few of the classical plays and see which ones you connect with the most and if you're lucky you might find a suitable monologue in there as well.

Whatever you choose – *do not negate the text*. When working on anything classical or even a modern classic you must truly understand, relish and enjoy the language; the words are your tools to communicate, you cannot ignore the style and importance of the text.

Once you have made your choices, you need to know how to work on the pieces. I deal with this in CHAPTER 6, 7 and 8.

CONTEXT OF MONOLOGUE

Firstly, I would like to address who you should be saying the monologue to… If you think about it, it doesn't make much sense to say the monologue out front, directly to the panel of people auditioning you. This seems to be what the majority of you want to do. Why? It doesn't make sense to me. Surely you want to create a make-believe world for three minutes. Certainly your character's world doesn't include the people auditioning you! Then why would you look them directly in the eye? How off-putting, if one of the people watching you started looking at their watch, or yawning or writing copious notes, or at worse pulling a face at what you were doing. How off-putting for you. Even if the monologue you choose was supposed to be directed at the audience, I would still advise not to take it directly to them. You might want to take it to the right or left of them or just above their heads, so your eyeline is still believable and you're not aiming it so high above their heads that you're straining your neck and looking unnatural. Of course if the preference is otherwise and you're instructed to look directly at the panel you must indeed comply regardless.

Secondly, you have to find the right context for the monologue. It doesn't always have to be the exact context of the play you took the monologue from. By this I mean, it doesn't always make sense to set it outdoors in the zoo if this is not referred to in the text and if it would be easier for you to believe it's set elsewhere. If the speech is to a large group of friends, just because it's written like that in the play it doesn't always mean you have to take it literally. I'm not suggesting you take it out of context if it doesn't make sense. It should be a choice that enhances what you do and should neither be random nor be made for the wrong reason. I believe that you can take audition speeches out of context and re-contextualise them because often you'll find the play you have taken the speech from requires a whole explanation and backstory to make sense of what just happened and what you're saying. If this is the case you've either chosen the wrong speech or you need to change its context to make sense of it. The right audition speech should be able to stand alone, have a beginning, middle and end and shouldn't have to come with a long explanation outlining what just happened beforehand.

How to choose the right monologue

- The speech should fit in well with your social, physical and vocal type. Yes, typecasting.

- If you look at your monologue and don't relate to it don't choose it.

- If the monologue only makes sense if you've seen or read the whole play, don't choose it unless you can change the context to make sense of it.

- I believe the best monologues should have an emotional arc. They should have a beginning, middle and end and should be an emotional journey of some kind.

- The best speeches pertain to something that's happened to your character and are not about someone else.

- I would stay away from any speeches that rant or are too verbose and just explain or report what's happened to you or anyone else.

Sometimes putting a speech in a different context can be as simple as making the character English instead of American and changing some of the cultural references or idioms to English ones: For example you could change a reference from 'Ninth Grade' to 'Year Nine', from 'Broadway' to 'Shaftesbury Avenue', from 'turtleneck' to 'polo neck'. American colloquial words that are pretty specific to certain Americans like 'lookit' or 'ascared' could be changed to fuller sentences like 'look at it' and 'I'm scared'; 'dollars, bucks and cents' become 'pounds and pence' etc. If you find yourself changing too many references in a speech, this might not be the right speech for you as you might as well rewrite it, which I wouldn't recommend. Failing that, you could retain the references and make it work for yourself by doing an accent or if you love the speech and want it to work in your accent, try to make changes that enhance the context of the speech.

I do believe in cutting speeches to make them shorter and cutting out the other characters' dialogue but it doesn't always work if you start cobbling too much. For example, if there's no real speech for the character you like and you are therefore taking bits of dialogue from various different pages and putting them all together to make one, unless you're expert at this, it can end up being a mishmash – you might as well look for a ready-made monologue.

SIGHT READING/COLD READING

I'm often surprised by how many actors seem to complicate the process of a simple sight-reading. On reading something aloud for the first time, you should neither over-characterize or under-characterize; both have pitfalls. It's not your place to do either, you should simply make sense of what you're reading and bring the character to life by making some simple choices. I don't agree with being in 'neutral' – the amount of students and young actors who have been told to do this alarms me. They have been told to go in to a reading or the first days of rehearsal and be very neutral in terms of character and voice. The premise is, you can then layer on top of this. I disagree and feel that although you should never over-define a character first off, you should always colour and bring something to the table by making clear, simple, initial choices.

I digress slightly, back to sight reading. Sometimes you're given a chance to read over the text silently to yourself – take full advantage of this.

☐ Scan the script and the first thing you should do is find a simple **objective/action**. For example, to get to the bottom of the truth, to flee the castle etc.

☐ Careful not to rush or to garble.

☐ Move your thumb down the page as you're reading so you can look up and still find your place when you look back down again.

☐ Don't under- or over-characterize, just try to play your **action** and be truthful to the scene.

If this is your weak area, you can easily practise this at home with almost anything from a bible, newspaper, magazine, play, novel…

I will discuss how to work on your speeches in CHAPTER 6, 7 and 8.

INDUSTRY AUDITIONS

PROFESSIONAL SIDES

Usually sides (pages of a script) come in a few days before your actual audition. If you're lucky you'll have them a week to ten days before and even earlier if you're really, really lucky. The reality is though, you only have a relatively short time to prepare your sides. What to do? The first thing I suggest, is to re-read the breakdown of your character because chances are, this might not be clear in the actual pages of text you've been sent. That will give you some clues as to the type of character you are supposed to be playing. Some breakdowns can be more detailed than others, but try and glean what you can and make some notes.

Due to the time constraint, here's what I suggest you do to prepare as well as possible. Even if you only have 24-hours notice try to resist just learning the lines – answering these simple questions could be a matter of twenty minutes and will make learning/delivering the lines so much richer.

☐ Base your character on someone (**personalisation**). This could be you, your younger self, or someone who fits the core of your character. You must always identify with your character. To find this go to step 2. If your character is based on a real person or true circumstances, then do the appropriate research. This will give you invaluable insights into the world, history and circumstances of the character.

☐ Write a shortlist of **inners** and **outers** and then extract 3 or 4 **outers** that sum up the **essence** of your character. Once you have done this, try to find a personalisation that encapsulates the 3 or 4 characteristics and you should have the essence of the character.

☐ Break down the text. Find your **objective** and then find **transitive/active verbs** for each beat. This could be on every line if the script is written as one-liners or if you have chunks of dialogue, find the beat on every change of thought.

☐ Find your substitutions for the situation of the scene. For example, the scene is dealing with your exasperation and frustration with your husband not taking you and your new-found job seriously – he is continuously deriding you. Even if you, as the actor, can't quite see why the character is getting so annoyed and wound up by it, you have to find a real-life or **'What if'** situation of something that does wind you up. If you want to get under the skin of the character you're auditioning for or playing you must find your parallel situation. It doesn't have to be like for like. You could use someone at work who always winds you up by talking too much or your mother who doesn't listen to you and misunderstands everything you say. Whatever scenario you decide on, it should help bring you closer to the situation of your character. If you can completely relate to your character then there's no need to look any further.

Please refer to CHAPTER 6 for more information on **personalisation, inners** and **outers, objectives, transitive/active verbs** and **substitutions**.

☐ Once you have done all the above, learn the script so that you don't have to hold it in your hand. Even if time is of the essence, it will make a good impression. I assure you, once you have put in the work above, memorizing the text will be much easier. If you really don't have time, make sure you're as familiar with the lines as possible, enough so you can look up at the person you're reading with. Please resist from going into panic mode and learning the lines immediately. This will not help you in the long run and will ultimately make it difficult to direct you as inevitably by drilling in your lines you will develop a fixed pattern and way of saying them, along with a fixed intonation that becomes almost impossible to shift. Doing the right sort of work on the character will make a big difference in the long run, even if it seems to be taking a long time – this will pay off.

☐ Dress the part for the character you're going up for. I'm not necessarily talking about full costume but certainly the essence of the character. If your character is supposed to be 'sexy', 'dishevelled', 'well dressed' or 'youthful' then make sure your dress sense reflects that. Depending on the level of audition, especially if it's a recall, you could even go to town and dress up all the way. I know an actress who on the morning of her audition, went to the hairdressers to get her hair groomed in the right way for the period of the character – she got the part and I have no doubt that taking the time so that she looked like the character was one of the factors that helped secure it. You can do a good audition but looking the part and making an effort can go a long way to showing the producers and director how serious and important getting this role is to you. Who knows, it could just swing it for you! In most cases, looking the part by wearing the right suit, hat, tie, jacket, dress, skirt, jeans, scarf or jewellery can only help increase your chances of gaining the part.

Self-Taping

This has become the most common way to audition for Hollywood TV and film projects. Embrace the process. Ultimately you're in control and can do this at home in front of a neutral background. You can do as many takes as you wish until you get the one you want. There are also pro companies that offer their services to tape for you if you haven't got a camera/tripod and someone to read with you.

Accents

To do one or not to do one? I think if the character you're going up for has an accent i.e. comes from a different country or just a different region, you should try and do the accent or dialect. I don't think it's something you should stress over. I don't think you should stop everything and get yourself a dialect coach. If you got the part there's every chance a dialect coach will be brought on board for the duration of the movie.

It might be useful to watch a film that's specific to the accent you need. If you're going up for a film that's set in, say, Texas and your general American accent is good but you're not sure about a Southern Texan accent, then watch a film that's set in Austin, Texas or anywhere within the state. Or if something is set in, say, South Africa or Liverpool, watch relevant films or documentaries. There is also a useful iTunes app, 'ooTunes', on which you can listen to any local radio station in the world – a valuable tool when trying to get an accent or the rhythm of another language or dialect.

The best way to approach an accent is to find a key phrase or saying that you can do quite well and perfect it – this can help you get into it quite quickly. It doesn't have to be perfect and definitely shouldn't take over what you're doing. It should enhance and just be a slight flavour of the accent. The last thing you want to do is let it overshadow the good work you're doing. I deal with this all the time and can't help but wince when the accent is not very good to the point that all I hear is how bad the accent is and it can sometimes seem like the person can't act. You definitely don't want that to happen. If there's a danger of that happening, don't overexaggerate the accent or don't use one at all. For example, if the character is, say, from Essex and you already have an Essex accent, there's no need to push your accent. The people auditioning you aren't deaf and will be able to hear that your accent is genuine and authentic so don't play it up.

Do you go in with an accent? I have seen both sides of this work and fail. I think you should judge the situation, the calibre of the audition and the route by which you got the audition. If it was through your agent or casting director, chances are they already know your nationality. I think the only time this could really work is if they don't know much about you. The only problem with this is, you could get the part but you won't be able to drop your accent or your invented backstory. It can be risky. I know an actor who went to a big audition for a major Hollywood film with a famous director. He landed the part as an American and had to keep the pretence for the entire shoot of the film. Not only that, he had to keep it up in between filming his scenes, as well as when the cast went out after each evening's wrap etc. He had to invent an entire backstory and life for himself. He got away with it but once the film was over he reverted back to his own North London accent. The director soon learnt that this actor wasn't really American and was furious at being duped. He never worked for that director again! I think the best approach to this would be to go in with your own accent and revert to the accent needed once you start reading the scene; that way they can hear your own accent and be impressed by your transformational accent. However the industry has changed so much in the last few years. There's a real influx of Brits now working in Hollywood who have perfected their US accents. It is not uncommon to gain a role as an American even though the casting directors, producers etc. are fully aware of your nationality.

How do you tackle an accent once you have the part? I would say, doing a convincing and sustained accent is a bit different to finding an accent just for the audition, which lasts only fifteen minutes or so. Once you have watched films and listened to various recordings, the best way to practise an accent is to try and use it as much as you can. You might feel embarrassed to do this at first but I suggest you initially use it around people you don't know that well or you don't know at all. Go into a nearby café and order a coffee and something to eat. Or go to your local supermarket and start by asking them questions: 'Where do you keep your fresh pasta?', 'When is the next delivery of your imported cheese?' etc. The more you get used to applying it the easier the accent will become. If you still feel awkward using it face to face, try making some phone calls to a utility company or a shop and once you see that they're taking you seriously, you will start to develop some confidence around your accent.

The aim is for the accent to feel natural, like it's second nature, and the only way that's going to happen is if you become comfortable using it. The last thing you want is to feel self-conscious and clunky. I wouldn't practise it on your actual script; that way you might lock in unwanted intonations, which results in bad habits. You can practise it on anything but your actual script/lines. As I mentioned before, once you find your key phrase for the accent it should be downhill from there as that should springboard you right into the heart of it and once found, you should be able to turn it off and on, and slowly but surely refine it so it ends up sounding sustained, natural and authentic.

Second-guessing and trusting your instincts

Never try to second-guess what the casting director, director or producers are looking for. All you can do is go prepared and make some intelligent and imaginative choices, which you then have to commit to fully. If you only make half-baked choices for fear they might not like you, then you are not showing them what you can do or bringing anything to the table. There's every chance they don't know exactly what they're looking for, therefore all you can do is make your informed choices and play them fully. That way, there's more chance they'll sit up and see the part in a different light.

Don't hedge your bets and play it so safe you actually rob yourself of auditioning to your full potential and instead of showing many colours you only show them one. Take a risk, follow through, commit and play it fully. That way, you won't leave the audition with regrets. Learn to trust your instincts. Don't be ruled by your head – the less you think the better, otherwise you will be working from the wrong place. You should do your very best and then try to forget about the audition and not mull, stew or fret over what you did or didn't do and what they thought or didn't think. Put it on a shelf, put it down to experience and move on – until you get the phone call from your agent!

5. YOU GOT THE PART, NOW WHAT? TECHNIQUE

Congratulations on getting the part! Whether it's lead or supporting in film, TV or theatre, I would imagine you still want to do the best job you possibly can and be truthful as the character. I think you must therefore try and do the right sort of groundwork by doing some research. If you can snatch and make some valuable time available, I feel you will reap the fruits of your labour. Of course this will depend entirely on how much time you have prior to your shoot or your first day of rehearsals. Even if you can't do everything I'm suggesting fully, I urge you to do as much as you can in order to build up your knowledge and understanding of the character and the world you're entering into. This will in turn give you security and confidence.

Let me introduce my 10 Acting Questions you must answer before approaching any role or audition:

1.) WHO AM I?
2.) WHERE AM I?
3.) WHEN IS IT?
4.) WHERE HAVE I JUST COME FROM?
5.) WHAT DO I WANT? (OBJECTIVES)
6.) WHY DO I WANT IT?
7.) WHY DO I WANT IT NOW?
8.) WHAT WILL HAPPEN IF I DON'T GET IT NOW?
9.) HOW WILL I GET WHAT I WANT? (CHOICES)
10.) WHAT MUST I OVERCOME? (OBSTACLES)

WHO AM I?

The first question is dealing with the type of person you are. You certainly will not be able to answer this question without reading the play a few times. Well, firstly, a good script should give you some initial information about your character. What other characters say or think about your character can also be very revealing. All this should be extracted and written down in a separate notebook. You can't expect a play, however well written, to give you all the information you need to know to develop a fully rounded character. Therefore the next stage would be to do research. The further back the period the more research you need to do especially if the play's set in another country. You need to find out what the history, economics, politics, music, art, literature, theatre, film, foods, fashion, religion might have been in order to know how you would have lived and what and who your influences were, just like you know in real life. The best source of information would obviously be the internet but also films of the era and images of landscapes etc. as well as museums, art and photographic galleries. This process is not an intellectual one so gathering too many facts and dates isn't going to get you that far. The more visceral your understanding the better, therefore films, music and images are going to enrich your creative process.

It's very easy to sidestep emotional content and feelings and just paint a very strong world and background for your character. Careful though, because if your character has a chequered past you need to be able to plant those painful memories in order to justify who you are in the play, film or TV series. If, for example, you're playing someone who is aggressive/violent and edgy, you need to find the justification in your biography, to know how you became that sort of person. Were you uneducated? Did you grow up in a dysfunctional home? Did you witness or experience abuse? Did that then affect your bad behaviour at home or school? What highlights, incidents can you invent or draw from in your own life that can add up to a profile similar to that of the character you have to play? The whole point of writing a character's backstory/biography is to give your character a life, a history, a profile.

2. WHERE AM I?

You might find in the script a description of the room you're supposed to be in, like the style and period of the furniture. What does it mean to you? Is your character supposed to be familiar with the surroundings? Is this the first time you've entered this room? Are you in a cosy cottage? A freezing barn perhaps? Or a sprawling mansion? Maybe a magnificent castle? Are you in your local park? Or just a familiar street? We usually behave differently depending on our surroundings. You need to think about your relationship with this environment, whether it's familiar or not, because this affects your physical life. For example, you wouldn't start walking around touching ornaments and putting your feet up if it wasn't your home. The country should also inform how you use yourself. If you're playing someone from a very cold, northern climate like Norway or Russia, you would behave very differently from someone coming from hot, Mediterranean climates like Italy or Spain.

3. WHEN IS IT?

With this question you need to consider: What is the year or century? This should certainly make a difference to the way you use yourself due to your surroundings and the way you dress. I think this is dealt with extremely well on film and TV sets, which often have wonderful and period-perfect costume and locales. Theatre tends to take more liberties due to financial restraint but sometimes, due to artistic interpretation, the play can be taken out of its original context and placed in another era or country. Whatever decisions have been made, you need to know **'When is it?'** in order to inform how you would behave re norms and mores of the period. People used themselves differently then – they didn't slouch or use modern gestures – and you must therefore reflect this in your physicality.

Whatever scene you're in, be it TV, film or theatre, you also need to know at what time the action is unfolding. It's usually more obvious for film and TV as the time of day is written into the script. It's less obvious for theatre. We all operate differently at various times of the day. Some of us are much more lively in the mornings, whereas others are more sluggish and come alive later in the day. Some people are definitely more nocturnal than others. We should be just as clear with our characters. You should make a conscious decision on your character's energy level in every scene.

4. WHERE HAVE I JUST COME FROM?

You have to know what your previous circumstances are. When you make an entrance on stage, I shouldn't think you've just stepped on stage from behind the curtain and it looks like you've just been waiting to come on. Even though that's the case, you should have worked out during the rehearsals where you would be coming from. Was it the bathroom? Having just brushed your teeth? Were you in the kitchen in the middle of baking an apple pie? Just coming back from the car after being stuck in traffic? Shopping? What is your state of being on your entrance? Does it tell you in the text? Has your director informed you of what he/she would like it to be? Or do you have to invent it? What's just happened in the scene before? How much time has lapsed from your last scene to your next entrance? Have you just had an argument? Have you just been proposed to? Whatever the situation, you should always know your previous circumstance at all times, even if you have to invent it. It's quite good fun and no entrance should ever be the same. Just think back to real life; do you always enter your house in the same way every night? No, your previous circumstance will have conditioned your mood.

When I'm directing, if I see my characters coming in from the outside with not a trace of a hat, coat, keys or bag, I will always question them, why not? Who ever comes in from outside with nothing? Unless you've come from the garden; in that case you might be coming in with a football, a drink, a packet of cigarettes.
I'm very big on bringing the outside (life) inside. I understand that it's a directorial choice, but I still believe you can try and make some choices as actors. It should never feel comfortable to come into a room empty handed. Why? Because we don't in life, so why should you do that in a scene?

5. WHAT DO I WANT? (OBJECTIVES)

This is a key acting question. Your want is your need, intention, motivation, **action**. You should never walk on stage or on set just to play a scene. You should always have some sort of **objective**. Often in a good script an objective is written into the scene. For example, to end the affair, to propose, to move out. Your **action** usually changes from scene to scene and it doesn't always have to be dramatic but you should always work out what you're meant to be doing. Sometimes you have very little dialogue and rather than just sit there listening you should give yourself a **physical action**. So if you're not interacting with another character you still should have a reason for being in that room. You could invent it or perhaps your director could give you one. It could be anything that fits your reason for being in that room from making a salad, to polishing your nails, to writing a letter, to setting a table. Even if you are pulled away from what you're doing, as long as you're doing something you've always got something to return to once you're no longer engaged in conversation. This way you won't look or feel silly on stage because you're not doing anything. You must have a life on stage, you must have a purpose for walking and talking, otherwise you are in danger of 'just acting', which is fake. Don't forget, you're trying to be truthful and multi-dimensional. No one in life usually comes into a room and either stands with their hands by their sides or sits with their hands in their lap and just talks so why should you!

6. WHY DO I WANT IT?

You must always have a strong justification for wanting and needing your **action**. Maybe in life we don't always have a strong justification but on stage, film and TV you always need one otherwise it makes a mockery of the drama unfolding. Most drama, especially theatre, is a **'heightened reality'** truth and not a **'naturalistic'** truth that we have in life and often see on the soap operas. Having a strong justification means you have a strong motivation.

7. WHY DO I WANT IT NOW?

The *'now'* gives you an immediacy, which is crucial in acting and in any drama. You must know why you have to get what you want now, not before, not later but *now*. Otherwise, if you're not that bothered whether you get the girl, boy, money, house or whatever the given circumstances might be, why should we sit through two hours of this drama or comedy unfolding? This does not mean urgency/**time stress**, it just means that what you do should not be rushed – you have to be present/in the moment.

8. WHAT WILL HAPPEN IF I DON'T GET IT NOW?

The stakes should always be high. If they're not, why bother? The consequences of not getting what you want should always be very important to you. If the high stakes are not clear in the play, you need to invent them, otherwise it will look as though you don't care about the outcome.

9. HOW WILL I GET WHAT I WANT? (CHOICES)

This question brings us on to how you break down a script. How do you know how to play the line as opposed to how you should say the line? There's a big difference. This question is all about how you play your intention. Once you've worked out what your **action** is (Question 5) you then have to work out your smaller action, which is called an '**activity**'. You need to find a transitive/active verb, a verb that is active. For example, to beg, to entice, to charm, to get sympathy. By playing these chosen activities you're trying to make the actor you're playing opposite feel something *specific* in order to further your **action**. This technique is also known as '**actioning**' your text. Have a look at the APPENDIX for an extensive list of transitive/active verbs. I don't believe it's helpful to try to break down every sentence you say, unless your script is written as just one-liners. I think realistically you should break your script into chunks, sections. Every time you have a change of thought you need to find a transitive/active verb that will affect the other person. These become your choices and inform how you play the line.

Please realise this technique is not about the emotional content of what you're saying or feeling but what you want the other person to feel *psychologically*. So, you have to think, how can I affect the other character, by doing what...? At this stage you should know who your character is and your choice of active verbs should be informed by your character choice and not your personal choice. If my character was a loving, open, sweet, sensitive young girl and my dialogue, for example, was 'I don't love you anymore, I think you should go', my verb will be determined by the above characteristics not by the actual line itself. Therefore, verbs like to plead, to get sympathy, to reason, should be chosen as opposed to verbs that might reflect another type of character like to demand, to threaten, to hurt. If a choice doesn't work in rehearsal then you can change it. Initially nothing should be set in stone.

I like to call this process 'scoring' your text; just like a musician or singer would rely on their score to know how to sing or play their song, this is how the actor works out how to play the monologue or scene. It's about trying to make the right choices using specific verbs to affect the audience or the other characters psychologically. Careful you don't get caught up in writing these verbs next to the dialogue and forget to play them. The whole point is, you work out what you want the other character to feel, and then you play it fully, otherwise you're just paying lip service to this technique – it will simply remain on paper. The challenge is in the execution. Finding the right verbs is initially time-consuming but once you have chosen them and tested them in rehearsal for a couple of weeks, not only will you have given your performance light and shade but also depth. It also means you won't fall into dreadful cliché performances because of concentrating on how to say your lines and on what you should be feeling and emoting. This technique allows the actor to be free and truthful without playing external emotions. It's really about what you don't say and trusting that **actions** speak louder than words.

10. WHAT MUST I OVERCOME? (OBSTACLES)

This is referring to the **inner** and **outer** obstacle an actor should always have. The outer obstacle is the resistance (usually the other character) to obtaining your **action**. The inner obstacle is your inner conflict, which you must always plant, even though it can change from scene to scene or even change within the same scene. There must always be a problem you're trying to overcome. If you think of yourself in life, you're never without an inner obstacle. For example, insecurity, fear, hate, love. On stage or screen if you don't plant the inners that's when you get a lot of actors shouting, over-emoting and sometimes just playing the aggression. If the inner obstacle were there, the anger, fear or hate for example, then you would have something to fight against in the scene instead of playing into it. Much more interesting! Thank God for inner obstacles – they are our inhibitors. Imagine a world where there were no inhibitors, everyone would say and do anything they wanted, there would be mayhem!

The mere planting of an inner obstacle will give you substance and depth. Just as in life, often the unsaid is more interesting than the said. If you think about it, we don't always say what we mean or mean what we say. Think back to socially awkward situations you've been in, like the time when you were introduced to your boyfriend's ex-girlfriend. Your outer was probably cool, calm, collected and polite whereas your inner was very likely insecure, jealous, hurt and upset. Or going up for a job interview or audition your outer might have been secure, confident and friendly whereas your inner may well have been insecure, nervous and fearful. Or meeting your girlfriend's parents for the first time. Your outer could've been secure, charming and confident, whereas your inner was probably insecure, apprehensive and vulnerable.

We have these ever-changing inner conflicts in life all the time. Sometimes they're extreme (hate, love, anger, fear) but often we don't show what's going on inside. However, it does condition how we use ourselves on the outside. That's why we're not black and white, we're multi-dimensional and pretty complex. Inner obstacles become our dilemmas and you must ensure you have them for every scene you do. Regardless of whether they change from scene to scene, they should always be there so you always have something inner to play against. If you plant the outer as hate and then the inner as pain, distress, guilt or frustration, it should make it impossible for you to fly off the handle with no limitations. If the inner is there it conditions your outer and certainly makes an interesting emotional tug of war.

Inner

Outer

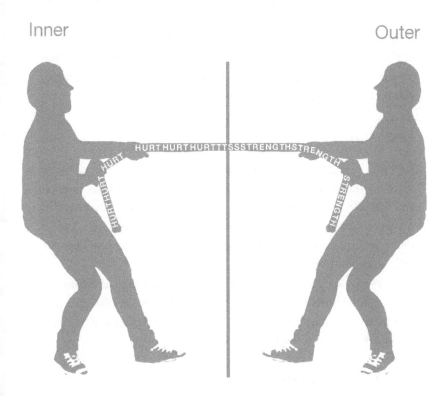

The same goes for crying. It's all very well finding the emotion and tears but if they take over the scene and it turns into something uncontrollable, weeping and blubbering all over the place with mucus dribbling out of your nose as well as being inaudible, this is not good, not good at all. You have gone too far and have not planted an inner. In real life when you're that upset and become so emotional, you are usually trying to overcome and fight the emotion off, rather than sink in to it; you would try to talk through your tears and would be constantly making an effort to recover as opposed to indulging more and more into it, wallowing in a sea of emotion. Your inner obstacle here would normally be one of shame, guilt, embarrassment, humiliation – this gives you something to play against.

This is also the case when you're playing drunk. Rather than allowing the condition to take over completely you should plant an inner obstacle; this could be pride, shame or embarrassment and that way you won't give way to typical 'drunk acting.'

I hope you can see the benefit and importance of inner obstacles; neglecting to plant them in scenes will almost definitely lead you down a path of 'obvious acting' whereas acknowledging your inner conflict will no doubt deepen your performance immensely.

RESEARCH

Research can take on many different forms. You can really go as in depth as you want or have time for. With the advent of the internet and with Google at your fingertips there's no excuse for lazy actors. In my day so many actors and directors had no choice but to go and sit for hours and hours in a library and plough through encyclopaedias making copious notes.

If you're playing a challenging role that is set in a different country or era you should be able to grasp the period. Or if you're playing a part that takes you out of your comfort zone, I suggest you break down your research to cover the following topics:

☐   **Political life and events**
Who's running the country? What are the political parties?
Is your country at war? Do they have troops in any countries?
Fighting a war away from home (WW1 – WW2 – Vietnam
– Korea – Falklands – Afghanistan – Iraq)? Were you affected
by the Great Depression (Wall St Crash of 1929)? The Berlin
Wall? etc.

☐   **Economic influences**
Find out the economic influences that would've affected you
growing up and as an adult. What is your social class? Were
you affected by the Cold War, famine, poverty, social services,
housing, unemployment?

☐   **Social events and activities / Pop culture**
Find out about the social group you would've been part of, the
kind of parties you would've gone to, dance halls, picnics, tea
rooms, restaurants/diners, home cooking, sports you would've

played and sport events you would've gone to, clubbing, internet, drive-in movies, fishing, bicycle riding, gambling, horse riding.

☐ **Music**
Find out what music was popular in the era and what kind of music you would've listened to as your character. You might want to source the music of the day to help you find the essence and spirit of the period.

☐ **Art and Culture**
Find out what fine and modern art was around and popular at that time and what kind of art you would've had hanging in your house.

☐ **Literature**
Find out what kind of literature was around and what was popular. What books would you have read growing up and what would you have read as an adult? You might also want to read some literature of the period to give you a better understanding of the world of the character.

☐ **Theatre/Music Hall/Film/TV**
Find out what kind of theatre, entertainment, film was around. What were you taken to see as a child? What would you have watched as an adult? What films/shows can you watch now to help you understand the period?

☐ **Food and Drink**
What did you eat and drink growing up? What foods were around? Who cooked and prepared your food? What were the local and traditional dishes? Desserts? Alcohol? Soft drinks?

☐ **Fashion**
What was the fashion of the day? What did you grow up wearing? In what style did your parents dress? How do you dress now? Including undergarments, accessories, jewellery.

☐ **Religion**
What is your religion? Are you religious? Find out about that specific religion. How has religion influenced your life? Do you go to Church or any other place of worship?

☐ **Playwright's life/Letters/Comments/Reviews**
This really only applies if you're researching a play. It can be very useful to learn about the playwright's early life and influences, read their letters and reviews. This can only help # a deeper understanding of the material you are performing.

I think it will be your judgement call to decide which topics are the most relevant and would give you a real insight into the period you are supposed to be living in. You should know your character's background almost as well as the era and country/town you grew up in.

You can cherry pick from the list but make sure whatever you research is thorough. There's no point skimming. Remember, this is not a school/college project; it's not going to be marked. It's for your benefit only. This isn't an intellectual or academic exercise and should be kept as practical and as visceral as possible. In other words, writing an essay or just printing off lots of stuff isn't necessarily going to help you. Watch a film/documentary, read a book, listen to music, make a scrapbook, see a show, go to museums, art galleries etc. This way you'll get a better understanding of the period.

WRITING A CHARACTER'S BIOGRAPHY

The first question is dealing with the type of person you are. I'm sure if I asked you that question, you would be able to tell me about your family background, your parents, grandparents, siblings. You would be able to describe them in detail. And the same would be the case re the house you grew up in, what it looked like, inside and outside. Your favourite room, what you could see out of your bedroom window, the smells you remember. Your earliest childhood memories, the kind of games you played, family holidays. Your education, favourite teachers, best friends, times when you got into trouble. Your first kiss, your first job, your likes and dislikes, influences, attitudes, anecdotes... All these good, bad, funny, interesting experiences shape us into who we are today. Most people don't walk around with all these memories on their back like baggage. They've already seeped into our being, our muscles, our subconscious, allowing us just to be, to exist.

When you play a character in theatre, TV or film you should know your character as well as you know yourself, so that character too can just exist and live. Of course that doesn't magically just happen, nor does it evolve only from rehearsals. As an actor you have to plant those memories, anecdotes and backstory so you have a fleshed-out, believable character. So, how do you build a character?

Once you've extracted your information from the script and completed your research, which can only get you so far, you have to use your imagination. This is your biggest tool for fleshing out the details you've gathered and bringing them to life. Don't underestimate the power and necessity of your imagination in the acting process. You can't use it without the back up of all the above nor can you use your imagination alone.

If you're playing a real-life character, try to source as much real-life information as you can. Whatever you can't find due to lack of material, you will have to fill in by inventing within the realms of the character's world.

LIVING THE CHARACTER

Should you get under the skin of the character you're playing by total immersion?

Does living the character 24/7 give you the edge over someone who doesn't? You might think I would answer 'absolutely' to these questions but I might surprise you by saying that I don't always think this is the way forward. There is something highly indulgent about having to totally *live* your character for a week or so in order to *be* your character. I do believe you have to 'own' your character and 'own' the stage you're playing on. Without paying lip service to 'playing' your character, you're actually taking ownership of it. For the most part I believe in using your imagination and of course your research to find 'who your character is'. I also believe that you can set up exercises or do **'An afternoon of'** or a **Private Moment** exercise to find many, many of your character's qualities.

A **Private Moment** is when you set up a morning, afternoon or evening for your character. You can choose 3 inner or outer characteristics you would like to explore through activities and objects. Give yourself a simple situation, i.e. an afternoon at home relaxing and you want to explore 'romantic, creative and idealistic'. The objects/ activities you might choose to bring these qualities out for your character might be to recite or compose poetry, to play piano, to paint a picture. You might want to light some candles and play music in the background to help create the right atmosphere. This exercise is not dramatic and should have no immediacy attached to it. It can be done at home to help you connect in more depth to your character.

I was recently working with the lovely Welsh actress Alexandra Roach who was playing the young Margaret Thatcher in the biopic *The Iron Lady*. Playing a real-life political leader who came from a completely different class and culture is very daunting. She was very intimidated by the enormous task ahead of her and asked me where she should begin. She was already reading Thatcher's autobiography, which was of course helpful, but how could she get into her shoes? She was scared to try out her newly found accent and said she felt uncomfortable and self-conscious. I suggested she put herself in the right environment; that she should dress up in a dainty dress with pearls and book High Tea at The Ritz. That's exactly what she did; both she and her boyfriend dressed up and totally role-played for a couple of hours. This took the edge off her fear and she not only enjoyed the afternoon but found her mojo and the courage she needed for the character.

Another example I can give – I was directing an American classic at RADA called *Tobacco Road* set in desolate farm country in Georgia in 1933. The characters were poverty stricken, living in tatters and literally had morsels to eat. The play centred on their family struggles. My studious group had done all their research and were raring to go. I suggested we transform our rehearsal room into a dirt road similar to where they were living. Soil was sourced immediately and hence our dusty rehearsal improvs began. What became the hardest for them to access was the fact that the characters were starving. After many rehearsals of not believing my well-fed, middle-class students, I suggested that if they wanted they could come to our morning rehearsals without eating breakfast so that they rehearse on an empty 'rumbling' stomach, making their craving for food more realistic. They all decided it was a good idea and actually it really gave them a sense of what it was like to feel starving. After that there was a much stronger truth even when they came in well fed they were still able to remember the feeling of hunger.

There was a rumour going around RADA that I had told my students to starve themselves in order to make them believable, 'wow how cool, how Method'. It's funny how an isolated exercise can cause such a flutter. My point here is that what I was setting up was a controlled environment where nothing was imposed. The difference between not eating over three hours as opposed to twenty-four is enormous; therefore the regulated improv is not in the least harmful.

On the other hand, I was once asked to direct the play *True West* by Sam Shepard. The play centres around two brothers and their sibling rivalry. On the first day of rehearsal I thought it would be a good idea to explore the relationship of the two brothers. The American actor turned up with three crates of beer. I casually asked him if they were real, hoping they were just bottles filled with water or a carbonated substitute. To my horror, I was informed they were 'real' beers that they were going to both drink throughout the course of the improv. My improvisations, if they're going well, can famously go on for 2-3 hours. I was not about to sit and watch two actors get drunk for real in front of me. I vetoed this idea immediately. The actors in turn were horrified at me for not allowing this to take place. They thought I was a 'Method' director and couldn't understand my reaction, no matter how much I explained to them that this was not my methodology. In this instance, they could have used their imaginations to find a substitute – a memory for when they've been drunk in the past. I can't believe that two young guys thought they had to literally get drunk in order to play drunk.

I must also stress you should never get so lost in a role that you can't shake it off after the performance or filming. I do expect to see a fully lived, believable, in-depth performance when I go to the theatre. I don't expect to see, however harrowing the play or role is, the actor getting so lost in the part that they can't muster a smile at the curtain call or the actor still in character after the play or filming is over and annoying everyone by carrying on talking in their character's accent/ voice. By the time you reach performance/filming level your accent should be fully evolved and you should feel confident enough to let it go once the film has wrapped for the day and the performance of the night is over.

FIRST PERSON

Once you're in rehearsal for stage or screen, I believe you should always refer to yourself as the character in the first person.

I am – I want – I do. To me there's something very fake about referring to your character in the third person, she – he – her – him. Who is that person? That person is you, right? Presuming you have done all your prep work, don't you think it's strange to turn up to rehearsal and after all that work of searching for, connecting and desperately trying to identify with your character, you now refer to them in the third person? I question it *all* the time; when actors say 'When she's going over to the church', I always ask 'Who's she? Who do you mean?', 'My character' and then I always say 'Well, who's your character?' and of course they always answer 'Me'. 'Well then', I say, 'why don't you refer to yourself as "I"?'

It's a very strange phenomenon, when actors and directors do this. It's almost as if there's an embarrassment to talk about your character as 'I.'To me it always comes across like a disclaimer – 'Oh well, it's not really me, it's my character…?' I think psychologically it's very wrong to separate yourself from the character; there's no point doing all the background research work and trying to bring the character closer to you if in one fell swoop you ruin it all by placing yourself outside of the role.

Some directors refuse to go along with this concept; they speak to the actor about their 'character' as if he or she is a third person – 'I think your character should move here…' etc. This doesn't help. I think there's a perception in the UK that talking in first person is too 'Method' and there's a real resistance, whereas in the USA this is commonplace.

I think the only time you shouldn't be in first person is right at the beginning when you've just landed the part, before you start rehearsals. Also, once you've finished your run or filming and you are doing a lot of press junkets and TV/newspaper interviews, it makes more sense to talk about 'her' or 'him' since you have completed the job.

THE MAGIC 'IF' AND YOUR IMAGINATION

I believe you have to use your imagination. This is the difference with so-called 'Method' acting where the belief is you have to 'live it to be it'. This could be very risky. The cliché example of this is, do you have to know what it is like to kill in order to play a murderer?

It's crucial for every actor to comprehend and be able to use Stanislavski's **'Magic If'**. You should think of it as **'suspension of disbelief'** when you're playing a role in a situation that's hard for you to identify with. You should ask yourself 'What if I was in that situation, how would it make me feel?' Let's take playing a murderer as an example. How do you play a murderer if you've never actually killed anyone in real life? OK, have you ever killed any insects? That annoying fly or mosquito that has been sucking your blood all night... You finally see it on the wall and you take the nearest shoe, take aim and then... swat it real hard on the wall. A direct hit – you see your blood running down the wall. Satisfying and rewarding, if somewhat violent. Why can't you draw on the 'Magic If' in this instance – what if the character you're meant to kill was that mosquito or wasp or cockroach?

What about if you have to deal with a grieving scene in which someone close to you is dying and you are fortunate enough not to have experienced losing anyone yet? How could you possibly feel connected if you haven't experienced loss? In this instance the 'Magic If' should kick in and you should use your imagination; 'What if' I lost my own mother, father, brother, sister, boyfriend, cat, dog... You would probably be devastated and you should use this 'What if' scenario to get the desired emotion, feeling and belief for the scene. You can apply this to almost anything you feel in the scene or play that is far away from you and hopefully by using the 'Magic If' the reality and truth of the scene should become much closer.

OBSERVATION/SENSE MEMORY

When you are on stage, in a film studio or on location playing one scene or many scenes you should have already worked out your relationship to your surroundings. The audience or other characters should not be able to see your homework.

I once got to sit in on a performance at the Actors Studio in LA many years ago and was shocked to see this actress make her first entrance opening the door, taking a deep inhalation to smell the air, starting to caress the door frame and the sideboard and practically everything in her path before she fully entered the room. Not only was this highly self-indulgent but an embarrassing display of 'demonstrating'. Who on earth does that? It was pure torture (not to say long and cringe-worthy). I guess that was her 'sense memory' – touching, smelling and feeling the place in order to show how much she missed, cared and loved the room she was walking into. I believe when you walk into a room for the first time, you're in the moment and not self-consciously showing how you feel about it. Your peripheral vision usually kicks in as soon as you walk through the threshold of the door without having to 'indicate'.

I believe there is a place for **sense memory** exercises but this should be homework or something you might want to explore in a class or workshop – not on the stage with a paying audience.

WEARING THE RIGHT CLOTHES

Whatever you like to call what you wear (costume/garments/wardrobe/dress/garb/apparel), it's essential that you find something for rehearsals that helps *you* feel more connected to the period. It's all very well being given your costume a few days before your 'dress' but what about the four weeks of rehearsal prior to that? If you're in a contemporary piece it probably doesn't matter as much, because chances are your own wardrobe won't differ a great deal from your character's. However, what if you're rehearsing a Chekhov, Strindberg, Ibsen, Shaw, Wilde, Coward, Molière or Shakespeare play? Surely rehearsing in jeans or sweatpants is not going to cut it for you; it will hinder you from finding the formality of the period or the elegance you need.

I don't mean that your rehearsal garments have to be period perfect, not at all, but wearing heels (even if they're not exactly the right period) can help you find the formality of the time and wearing a bow tie can make you feel more connected to the 1930s. Accessories can really help – shawls, fans, winged collars, cufflinks, hats, braces, earrings – as well as undergarments like corsets, petticoats, long johns etc.

THE FOUR SEASONS

We tend to use ourselves differently in the colder months than we do on hot, muggy summer days; we adjust according to the season. Often this is reflected by our mood and what we wear. For example, in winter we bundle and wrap ourselves up in warm clothing to keep cosy and comfortable. If you live in a Northern climate or observe people in countries like Scandinavia or Russia, where winters are extremely harsh, you will notice that the psyche of their citizens is a lot heavier, darker and more closed than their Mediterranean counterparts who live in sunnier, brighter countries like Italy, Spain and Greece.

However cliché this may seem, you can't separate climate and culture as one reflects the other. In countries like Sweden, Norway and Finland temperatures can reach lower than 30 degrees Celsius. The average daylight in winter is around 6 hours and in some Northern regions there's no sun for about 2 months. Living in that sort of climate can make you more insulated and want to spend as many hours as possible inside, around a warm open fire. It's no wonder that people from Northern climates are known to be introspective and private. Whereas in the Mediterranean and southern hemispheres, where the climate is hot, you tend to find people a lot warmer and more open due to spending a lot of time outdoors socialising.

CULTURAL DIFFERENCES

Don't underestimate the differences in how people function in different countries. I've just talked about how climate can affect you. I've been fortunate to work in many different countries, therefore I got a chance to observe and work with different cultures first hand. No matter what country I was in, I always noticed it was very hard for actors not to bring their own cultural rhythm and physicality to characters from another country/culture who would've used themselves differently.

For example, when I worked with Swedish actors on Arthur Miller, their pace was so slow you could drive cars through their pauses. American tempos are much faster – they had to find quicker impulses in order to get closer to the American rhythm. I found myself frantically clapping out a fast beat in between their long Swedish pauses in order to energise their slow and thoughtful pace.

Let me take one of my extreme examples of working on Shakespeare in Israel. This wasn't the case of trying to make Israeli actors English but trying to get them to understand they would have to find another way of using themselves physically, if they wanted to get closer to finding truthful characters who lived in Elizabethan England. This would mean trying to physically move in a more formal manner as well as gesticulate less. My quirky method there was to tie their hands behind their backs to inhibit their expressive Middle Eastern physicality. Israelis by nature are very emotional and passionate, not dissimilar to, say, the Italians, Greek or Spanish who no doubt will have this same issue.

Wherever you're from you shouldn't ignore the fact that Elizabethans didn't talk with their hands and weren't very tactile. You need to try to understand the culture and era you're in and not bring the role right down to you and your contemporary mannerisms. You, the actor, have to reach for the character and as I've talked about earlier, it doesn't just happen. You have to realise in this instance that Elizabethans were more conventional and language was the biggest tool of communication. Therefore, in order to play Shakespeare, especially the more formal characters (Queens, Kings, Princesses etc.) you have to change the way you use yourself and address the question **When is it?**. I'm clearly not talking about a modern version of Shakespeare which is set in the 20th century; that would still need you to ask the question but the answers and outcome would be different.

6. HOW TO DEVELOP
A CHARACTER IN DEPTH

Actors often say the reason they're attracted to acting is that it's an excuse to roleplay. Young actors often talk about wanting to 'hide behind' a character as it gives them the freedom to be someone else for a couple of hours. I call this process 'transformation'. I also like to think it's not so much a case of hiding behind a character as 'becoming' the character. This doesn't just happen by turning up to rehearsals day after day waiting for the character to jump out at you as you say the text, nor should you expect the director to give you your character.

To find a character you have to make certain choices about who they are by looking at the clues you get from the play. You also have to research, write a biography and, lastly, have a discussion or many discussions with your director. I have talked about all the above at length in CHAPTER 5 'Who am I?' OK, so what do you do once you've read the play a few times and extracted everything that the playwright and other characters have said about you? You've done your research and written a biography… Now what? You can't act your biography can you?

For example, if you take yourself, you know who you are (or at least you do to a certain extent). You know where you were born, the house you grew up in, your relationship with your parents, siblings etc. You know what your education was like, you remember family holidays, you have good memories, bad memories… All your past experiences have shaped you to who you are today (for good or for bad). My point being, in life we take all this for granted. Just think of yourself walking into your flat – you're just 'being' yourself. When you talk to a friend, you're 'being' yourself. This is exactly what we want for your character. You need to strive towards 'being' your character not 'playing' your character. Therefore when you've been cast as the doctor, lawyer, femme fatale, villain or cuckold, you should aim to be a fully rounded character who's living and breathing and who has good qualities and bad qualities. We should not see you 'playing' the obvious mannerisms you think a doctor, lawyer etc. should possess.

If you set out to play the villain, bitch or overbearing mother, you're making a comment and a judgement you might hear from other people watching the movie or play; you should never perceive your character as such – you must have empathy for your character and be able to fully justify your actions. If you comment on your character in your acting – show us you're a bad person or a silly person – you are signalling this to us and in fact you become a cliché. Just think about it, no bossy person thinks they're bossy, no bitch thinks they're a bitch so why should you set out to play one! Everybody else around you might think that but you shouldn't.

The only way you're going to avoid doing this is knowing who your character is and developing 'empathy' so that you can transform – in other words, own your character by living your character.

(i) OUTERS AND INNERS

I believe if you're trying to depict a truthful three-dimensional character then you need to recognize that human beings are made up of inner and outer characteristics. Characteristics are 'a feature or quality belonging typically to a person, place or thing and serving to identify it'. For example, if I just take the outer characteristics/qualities of an archetypal person this is what it might look like:

OUTER
Secure
Open
Happy
Kind
Warm
Generous
Witty
Fun-loving
Intelligent
Loving
Down to earth

If the buck stopped there we might have a problem, as this is not a true depiction of a person. If I was to relate this back to a character and these were the only characteristics you put down, I might say you have a caricature on your hands – one-dimensional. If the list of your archetypal person looked more like this, however, I would say this was closer to the **make-up** of a human being:

OUTER	INNER
Secure	Insecure
Open	Shy
Happy	Melancholic
Kind	Kind
Warm	Lonely
Generous	Selfish
Witty	Bitter
Fun-loving	Jealous
Intelligent	Thoughtful
Loving	Romantic
Down to earth	Idealistic
Confident	Vulnerable

This is by no means a definitive list but as you can see the **inners** are almost all contrasting to the **outers**. This gives us depth and is what makes us human. Hopefully we have more than twelve characteristics in our make-up – I would imagine over fifty. You can be the same outer as you are inner but the more opposites you can find the more interesting and diverse this makes you as a person and as a character.

I always think it's quite a good exercise to write down your own characteristics before you tackle your character's. This will make you think about yourself because you have to do it as objectively as you can. Although this is not an easy task, I highly recommend taking the time to do it. Think of it as a working list, a list in progress. You don't have to complete it but think of adding to it, amending it over the months, years. As we are ever-evolving humans, learning, growing and developing all the time, so should your list. The more you know about yourself, the better actor you will be! Don't forget, the list needs to be as objective as possible otherwise it defeats the object of the exercise.

Compiling a list for your character is slightly trickier as the only thing you have to go on is the play/screenplay. Sometimes you don't learn an awful lot about your character. Then what? Well, it's a combination of a few things. Since all you have is the script, this has to be your first port of call. You need to take down everything you learn about your character; but here's the thing, just because your character has an emotional breakdown, let's say, or turns aggressive doesn't mean these translate into workable characteristics. These are what I call '**circumstantial situations**'. Just because you broke down or got angry, it doesn't mean that's the type of person you are. Circumstance played a part in this, so you have to be able to separate circumstantial situations from the actual make-up of the character.

For example, let's use an imaginative real-life situation. You're out having a good time with a friend, walking around all the shops, having a good laugh. You decide to go into a restaurant and order lunch to treat your friend who's unemployed and doesn't have much money. As you're about to pay for it you discover your wallet/purse is gone – you lost it or it's been stolen, either way all your money and credit cards are gone. Perhaps you get upset. What if the café owner doesn't take pity and insists on you paying and perhaps even accuses you of making up the story in order to get a free meal. You get into an argument, perhaps even get aggressive, cry hysterically. Let's say someone was watching all of this, was then asked to write your outer characteristics and wrote all the emotional ones down:

OUTER
Aggressive
Emotional
Violent
Worried
Argumentative
Defensive
Sad
Upset
Hysterical

This surely would not be a true list as it's based on feelings and circumstance. Therefore, when you're reading a script you have to be a bit of a detective and not only look at what happens to the character in the play but how you imagine that character to be when you don't see them i.e. when they go offstage or off-camera. You need to think of them outside of those two hours in the play or film. What are they like then? If we're saying that a good play or film is based around something heightened that often occurs in the space of a few hours, what are they like on a normal day when the cops haven't been called in or they haven't been proposed to... What then? You need to look at the nature of the person rather than their reaction to events and this will help in piecing the character together.

Key Points:

- **Keep it objective**
  You should write your characteristics as the actor – if you're too subjective while playing the character this isn't going to help you.

- **Don't comment or judge**
  Characteristics should not be negative. For example, if your character is bossy, you shouldn't write 'bossy' down – this is a comment. Other people might think your character is bossy but you shouldn't think that. As the actor, you may believe your character is particularly unpleasant or nasty but you shouldn't have that in mind as the character. You have to find a way to empathize and like your character otherwise you will be in real danger of judging them.

- **No emotions or feelings**
  Characteristics should NOT be about emotions i.e. angry, worried, upset, frustrated, hurt, guilty.

- **No reactions**
  Characteristics should be made up of the nature of person you are rather than made up of reactions.

Here are some examples of characteristics (for a full list have a look at the APPENDIX):

Ambitious	Generous	Stubborn
Aggressive	Genuine	Sentimental
Artistic	Imaginative	Sincere
Aware	Insecure	
Careful	Lazy	Talented
Charming	Loyal	Tenacious
Curious	Maternal	Trusting
Emotional	Opinionated	
Fragile	Organised	Understanding
Fearful	Perceptive	Warm

Avoid reactions and feelings like:

Hurt	Unbalanced
Angry	Enthusiastic
Confused	Excited
Uninterested	
Interested	Eager
Disturbed	Concerned

So now let me take you through the process of 'Building a Character'. As I mentioned, if you're trying to depict a truthful three-dimensional character then you need to recognize that human beings are made up of inner and outer characteristics. A provisional list of **inners** and **outers** is the next phase as later on, when you will be breaking down your script, these will inform the choices you make on your **activities**.

The first character I will examine with you will be Catherine from Arthur Miller's *A View from the Bridge*. We learn that Catherine is a young, typical teenager living in Brooklyn in the 1950s. Even a somewhat uncomplicated teenager who shows an outwardly secure face to the world has to have contrasting characteristics to bring Catherine to life.

OUTER	INNER
Secure	Insecure
Happy	Thoughtful
Sensitive	Fragile
Naïve	Vulnerable
Warm	Warm
Dependent	Independent
Carefree	Fearful
Optimistic	Sentimental
Romantic	Idealistic
Loyal	Loyal
Kind	Kind
Mature	Immature
Spontaneous	Childlike
Educated	Daydreamer
Trusting	Jealous
Loving	Loving
Imaginative	Vibrant

Here's another example of a slightly more complicated character, Russian aristocrat Lyubov Ranevskaya from *The Cherry Orchard* by Anton Chekhov.

OUTER	INNER
Extravagant	Generous
Romantic	Romantic
Escapist	Idealistic
Poetic	Poetic
Charming	Lyrical
Kind	Kind
Subjective	Sentimental
Sincere	Sincere
Enthusiastic	Emotional
Unpredictable	Irresponsible
Fantasist	Unrealistic
Frivolous	Frivolous
Impetuous	Sensitive

Gentle	Gentle
Loyal	Loyal
Unaffected	Unaffected
Confident	Secure
Optimistic	Optimistic
Vulnerable	Open
Capricious	Weak
Lively	Imaginative
Demonstrative	Passionate

Here's another example from *Roberto Zucco* by Bernard Marie Koltès based on the real-life story of a psychopath.

OUTER	INNER
Secure	Insecure
Charming	Insincere
Opinionated	Bitter
Manipulative	Ambitious
Sensitive	Fearful
Gentle	Aggressive
Resourceful	Scheming
Tolerant	Lonely
Controlled	Vulnerable
Good-natured	Envious
Rational	Calculated
Simple	Naive
Polite	Sadistic
Sincere	Negative
Tenacious	Volatile
Articulate	Repressed

Now the lists of characteristics are all very well and good but how do you use them in a practical way? The most common mistake actors make is that they want to show the whole character at once. This is impossible to do, just as it is in real life. Take a first meeting with someone you haven't met before. I guarantee within the first few minutes you would've gleaned their 'essence' and decided this is a very sweet person or very gentle, insecure, confident, intense, intellectual, witty. It doesn't mean to say that the person doesn't have other facets to their personality, it just means those other qualities are lying dormant until they're with someone who they do have a history with, like their mother, boyfriend/girlfriend or work colleague. The characteristics dominant now might be playful, emotional, immature, vulnerable, jealous or irritable. It doesn't mean you're a different person it just means we use different sides of ourselves depending on our relationship/dynamics we have with the people around us. As actors we have to work out the whole of the character first, rather than just select a few characteristics that are strikingly obvious and might even be cliché.

NEXT STAGE: HOW TO FIND CHARACTERISTICS

I suggest after you have a working list of inners and outers to now extract three or four that you think represent the **essence** of your character; the qualities that are the most dominant when you meet someone for the first time. Outers are usually easier to access than inners, as inners are more hidden so I don't advise using them at this stage. Let's say you pick the following as the **overriding characteristics**:

Sociable
Charming
Confident
Ambitious

This doesn't discount the rest of your list it's just the best starting place on which you can base your character. Once you have your four characteristics, you then have to ask yourself – How far away are these characteristics from you? If they're not very far from you at all, you might well be able to base the character on yourself, your younger self or perhaps even your older self. In this case you're lucky to be able to identify with the character so easily and you should then start focusing on developing the inner life of your character, which you set up in the same way as outers.

What if your overriding characteristics are further away from you? Let's say:

Organised
Impatient
Religious
Proud

Firstly, you have to find a '**personalisation**'; i.e. someone you know to base the character on. Start with your close circle: your mother, father, brother, sister, uncle, aunt. Then spread the circle to cover your cousin, best friend, co-worker. Then widen the circle to cover politicians, someone from history or even a famous actor.

This is a great starting place to try to find your character. Of course you will be filling in all the **inners** as well, but for now we need a real person to base these four characteristics on. It doesn't mean to say the person you're basing them on doesn't have other qualities but remember we're only focusing on the overriding ones. I will be talking about **personalisation** in much more depth in CHAPTER 6(ii).

I would like to stay focused though on characteristics. Let's assume you have found a personalisation for the character but three out of four of the above characteristics are far away from you; impatient, organised and religious. If these are not really in your armoury you need to bring them up to the surface in order to play a character that is ruled by them. We are going to explore how you can use objects and music in isolated exercises to help you find these different qualities.

Being impatient

First let's take 'impatient'. Assuming this characteristic is far away from you or something you don't experience very often, you have to think back to a time in your life when something made you feel impatient. I say 'something' because if it's 'someone' then of course you can't set it up as an Object Exercise.

Aim

You need to find an object or an activity that you think will make you feel impatient. It will be the 'doing' i.e. working with the object or engaging in the activity that will give you the desired characteristic you're after:

Examples of activities

Wiring a plug
Sewing
Doing a puzzle
Solving maths
Trying to play an instrument

Tip

Impatience is close to frustration – careful not to let it tip too much in that direction. If it does, stop the exercise and tweak accordingly.

Being organised

This characteristic is simple to set up. I would take a file, a ring binder, a clothes drawer or kitchen drawer, a section of your wardrobe etc. that needs organising. Sort all your college papers or accounts, throw away out of date receipts, colour code, fold your clothes etc.

Aim

You should choose one task that will sustain you. The desired effect is to feel methodical by being orderly. You should get great satisfaction from being organised.

Tips

Don't give yourself too much to organise otherwise this could tip you into feeling overwhelmed and inadequate.

Don't multi-task. Don't involve anyone else. Keep it simple.

Test

If you have a monologue or a scene, try to rehearse a bit and see if the last 30 minutes or so has paid off.

Being religious

The next characteristic you will be testing is religion. This exercise has similarities with **Private Moment** which I have already discussed in CHAPTER 5.

If you're not religious and your character is, let's say, a devout Christian, you have to ask yourself what would make *you* feel religious. Going to church? Saying the Lord's prayer? What about reading passages of the bible? Intellectually this might sound right but in reality you won't really know unless you try. I would say, these actions alone might not make you feel like a religious person but what if you set up a sustained exercise that could help draw you in closer to feeling devout?

The following exercise is set up to give you an intense religious sensation. You can choose to do some of the following activities separately; how long you spend on each one will really depend on whether you connect with it. If one section works better than another, then have the courage to stay with it a bit longer.

There's no point rushing this experience – allow yourself enough time to explore and make sure phones are off and no one will walk in and disturb you. Allow yourself to enjoy the sensation and don't block yourself in any way.

The following set up is just an example to inspire you and show you how far you can go in order to explore a characteristic using objects and music but please don't feel you have to do everything mentioned.

Examples of activities

Over the next few days, gather as many religious artefacts as possible i.e. crosses, Virgin Marys, bible, candles, incense etc.

Set up your bedroom or living room as a mini chapel. Close all windows, blinds, curtains and safely arrange as many candles and incense as you can to make it church-like.

Set up a mini-altar where you can put a cross and various religious icons including pictures of Christ.

Wear a cross. Hang various crosses around the room. Have a cross prepared that you can hold.

Make sure you have a bible and a hymn book. Pre-select certain passages, prayers and hymns that you can sing and recite.

Dress yourself in either black or white. Girls could even dress nun-like if that would help and guys as priests. Guys can easily do this by wearing a white shirt backwards so the buttons are at the back and the collar is at the front. Once you put a plain black jacket over it this should give you a sense of feeling like a priest.

Play religious Gregorian music in the background.

Once all this is set up, kneel before your altar and start reciting aloud some prayers or passages. Every so often you can cross yourself.

Aim

You should be aiming to tap into something spiritual. You should be completely immersed and transported which should leave you feeling serene, tranquil and will get you close to a religious experience.

Tips

Have in your mind something or someone specific to pray for – a family member or friend who's sick, a job you want etc.

You could substitute pictures of Christ for pictures of someone you love. Or have them alongside.

If you start to cry, don't fight it, allow the emotion to be there. Don't stop the exercise, unless you feel this is the natural end.

I advise to do this exercise for a minimum of 30 minutes and a maximum of an hour.

Test

Give yourself a small task around the house, like tidying up or doing the washing up, testing whether the feelings of serenity and religion haven't dried up.

If you have a monologue or a scene, try to rehearse a bit and see if the last 45 minutes of religious immersion has paid off.

Being aggressive

Let's take 'aggression' as another example of a characteristic you want to explore. You will need to find a fairly big studio space or perhaps even an open-air space like a garden. Some of these examples are trial and error and there for you to tweak but here's what has worked in the past with my students.

I would start by finding some loud music. Heavy metal has a very strong pulse running through it and its lyrics tend to be angry and hostile so at a loud volume it could definitely feed into your quest to find aggression.

Next I would find a sustained activity or a few stations of activities that you could have pre-setup like:

Some pillows/cushions that you can hit on the ground or stationary furniture like a couch.

A hammer and nails with various pieces of wood standing by to bang into the wood.

An axe and some logs.

Some sturdy sticks to bash on trees or on the ground.

A pair of boxing gloves and a punch bag.

I must stress all the above was carried out under my supervision and I would strongly advise that these activities be set up safely ensuring there's nothing too close by that could get smashed or damaged along the way; take care not to hurt yourself.

Once your sustained activity or your various stations are in place put on the music; if you can sing along or shout above the music this should help. Aggression usually comes quite quickly (after 5 minutes or so), along with a feeling of fury and exhilaration.

Aim

To find inner and outer rage that is otherwise hidden in everyday life by surrounding yourself deliberately with loud aggressive music and strong physical activities.

Tip

This exercise can sometimes trigger deep hidden emotion and can end up with you shaking and crying. Don't be scared by it. This can sometimes happen if aggression is an emotion you have buried for many years. If it's overpowering, just allow the feelings to manifest.

Test

You don't have to channel it into doing an activity if it's an overwhelming experience. The fact that you've allowed yourself to access it is an achievement in itself. If you feel up to it, you can give yourself a simple activity around the house or garden – tidy up the mess you may have made or just put away the things around you. This emotion is too big to go straight into your desired scene or monologue; I would wait until the feelings are less raw.

If it's too difficult to rehearse outside of the rehearsal room don't worry, in the next section I will talk about using **triggers** and how to transfer what you have found in the exercises into rehearsals and performance.

Of course I have only used a few examples of ways to isolate characteristics that are far away from you, but there are hundreds to be tapped into. Hopefully I have inspired you to explore deeper into yourself and your character, bringing characteristics closer to you so they can be part of your armoury and should be only a scratch away.

(ii) PERSONALISATION / SUBSTITUTION / ENDOWMENT

PERSONALISATION

What is **Personalisation**? This is a technique, which if you use correctly will unlock the door to characterization and the world of the play or film you're in.

Basically, you need to find a real person who you can base your character on. So, you have a character that you are auditioning for, or maybe you have the part already – Then what? You need to be able to relate to your character, otherwise how can you play her/him.

Almost the first question I will ask you is, who can you base the character on? What image can you use?

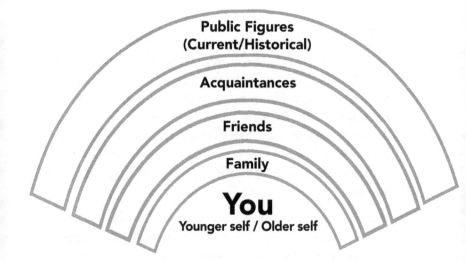

Yourself? Your younger self? Your mother? Father? Sibling? Grandparent? Cousin? OK, no one from your family. What about the next circle? Best friend? Schoolteacher/master? Friend of friend? Or the next circle? The guy you always see from afar at your local pub? The shop assistant from your local supermarket? Or maybe it's someone you've never met before? You can use the image of someone you don't know: that actor who you've seen in films or TV? That politician, or political leader, current or from history. In some circumstances you could even base your character on a picture that you found that embodies the image of what you need for your character.

My point is, you don't need to physically know the person you're basing your character on *but* you always need to have an image of the person you're playing. Once found this could open up the door to connecting to your character.

Personalising doesn't mean imitating, it means using the image of a person in order to play him/her: authoritative, outrageous, moral, refined, calculated, bossy, etc. etc. This in turn can really free you up and bring you close to the essence of your character.

Where do you begin?

In CHAPTER 6(i) I talk about choosing the 3 or 4 overriding characteristics; these become the basis for finding your personalisation. If you were working from your full list of qualities it would be near impossible to find a person that has every single one, therefore boil it down to 3 or 4 predominant ones. So the question you would be asking yourself is: Who do I know whose essence is sweet, soft and demure? Bold, feisty and jealous? Strong, confident and aggressive?

Once you have found the personalization that is the nearest to those characteristics, you need to test it. Either read your scene or your monologue – did it change you? If not, it could mean it either wasn't the right choice or you weren't using personalisation correctly. I can identify instantly if you're not using it but if you feel it's not working, you can either find another one or be brave enough to use the image of the person you're testing. personalisation is instantaneous and, once you think you found the right person, the results are *immediate*. You should not have to think this through or imitate, it either brings out the overriding characteristics or it doesn't. This can feel incredibly releasing especially if you're looking to find a character very different to you. It can really free you up and once you have tested it, it should always work. You might need to consciously remember to use it but once you've done this a few times you need to trust it's there, allow it to be there and focus on being in the moment.

How to use personalisation correctly?

The biggest misconception when it comes to personalisation is when actors try to combine different heads and bodies and personalities into one personalisation. Impossible – trying to use the personality of your dad and the body of your friend. Yikes, don't even go there. This technique is very immediate and the minute you try to create something that you have to think about, forget it. As I mentioned, this is also not about imitation. You should not be trying to imitate the person you are basing your character on. Remember, it's the essence you're looking to capture. For example, let's say the characteristics are extrovert, charming and funny and let's say your best friend is exactly like that; just thinking of them and using their image should immediately bring out those characteristics. However, if you personally don't know anyone that's like that but you're a big fan of, say, the comedian Peter Kay, or Amy Schumer, then by using his or her image you should get the same outcome. If not (perhaps it makes you too sardonic and sarcastic), then adjust your personalisation, it's as simple as that. It's worth spending some quality time choosing the right one as this can save you weeks and weeks of distress at not having found the character. Of course the buck doesn't stop there because once you've found the right personalisation you will need to fill in and deepen your character with a history/backstory, which I talk about in CHAPTER 5.

Of course if your character has some sort of cathartic experience or breakdown or something happens in the play or film that shows a completely different side of them, you'll need to find another personalisation that reflects that change.

How to personalise other characters

Once you have found a personalisation for your character, you should try and work out the different relationships and attitudes you have with all the different characters you're in contact with throughout the play/movie. If you think about real life, we talk to people differently depending on the kind of relationship we have with them – close, loving, distant, estranged, trusting, formal etc.… Therefore work out what relationship you have with each character and then choose a personalisation that fits that relationship.

Let's take for example a common occurrence in plays, films, TV series; you have to be in love with your girlfriend/boyfriend/husband/wife/lover. Now let's take some extreme examples:

You have one day's filming on a feature film or TV series and you don't have the opportunity to get to know your love interest.

You're in a long-running play and you can't bear your love interest.

You're in a play/film/TV series and you think your love interest is a lousy actor.

You're in a play/film/TV series and you've had a real-life affair with your love interest but have since split up acrimoniously.

Then what?

It's extremely dodgy territory to use the actor as the character, even if you think they are attractive, a good actor or you are in a real-life relationship with them. Of course it helps a lot but my advice to you would be to personalise at all cost.

Ideally you should find someone in your own life that you love. It doesn't have to be like for like, you don't always have to find the absolute parallel – boyfriend, girlfriend, husband or wife. What if you've never been in love, in a relationship or for that matter married…? You do have to find someone you love though. This could be your mum, dad, sibling, best friend. As long as whomever you use brings out the right feelings in *you* for the scene. For that you need to work out the *essence* of your relationship and how you're meant to feel towards the other person. If it's one of love, care and trust, you could use a parent, sibling, even a pet. Or if it's one of lust, attraction and desire you could use a real-life partner or even a film star or singer you're attracted to. Doing this can put you in the zone much more, rather than just relying on being attracted to the actor you're playing opposite. If you are a man in a love scene with a woman but are only attracted to men, I would personalise her as a guy you care about and vice versa. Obviously this can also apply to friendships or acquaintanceships as well as having to hate or fear another character. I strongly suggest you work out a personalisation for every single character in your script.

Surroundings/Situations

You must also personalise the situation. This is always neglected and it's one of the first questions I ask an actor. You must find your parallel situation.

Let's take the situation in *Miss Julie* by August Strindberg. Set in Sweden in 1874, Miss Julie, an aristocrat, has a torrid affair with her footman, Jean, and is so fearful of her contentious situation (Master and servant) that they plan to run away. Worrying he now has power over her, Miss Julie gets very distressed when she realizes that she has ruined his future and her own is also doomed. They are convinced running away is their only hope but fear of being trapped and the hopelessness of their situation overwhelms them, when Miss Julie asks Jean if there is any way out, he hands her his razor blade so that she can commit suicide. As she walks through the door at the end of the play, we can only imagine she ends her life.

It's extremely hard in the 21st century to imagine the high stakes of this situation and that it's the end of the world to sleep with someone from another class. Therefore you would have to raise the stakes high enough to make this 19th-century reality shocking for the 21st Century so that you believe that the only way out is to end your life. How can you personalise this situation? What substitution or parallel could you use to make this a believable situation for you? What situation could shame you enough that you felt the only option would be to run away…?

Could you imagine that if you came from a good middle- or upper-class family and you got heavily into drugs, the only option you had was to hide away...? What if you were involved in something dishonest/ illegal – theft, forgery, embezzlement...? Or something scandalous like an affair with someone who is already married and is in the public eye? You need to think of a 'What if' situation that you can believe and use as a substitute for Miss Julie or any other character that's in a situation that's far away from you.

You must remember, in trying to find a 'What if' situation you must think 'It's not what you *would* do but what you *could* do.' That should open up your imagination significantly.

Monologues

You mustn't neglect personalisation in monologues. You need to personalise yourself, the situation and the characters you're talking to even if they're not there.

Monologues to an audience

Soliloquies or Shakespeare plays, in fact anything you need to direct to the audience, should also be personalised. You can personalise the audience collectively as one person. It should be 'as if' the audience is your boyfriend or mother or best friend. You decide what relationship you need to have with the audience – friendly, close, trusting – then think of one person in real life that you have that relationship with and that should help you connect with them.

You should then make a choice as to what you want them to feel at any given time – to involve, to get sympathy, plot, scheme, befriend.

Why personalise?

I have sometimes had worried students come up to me in the past panicking about the difficulty they have in trying to personalise Shakespeare or anything classical. They felt scared to use a contemporary personalisation, thinking it would take them away from the period they were trying so hard to believe in. It's a good question in a way, but let me set the record straight. Personalisation is not there to alienate you from the period you're supposed to be in, on the contrary it's there to help you believe in your character's situation and world even more.

IMPORTANT

You need to remember, Personalisation changes **YOU** and not the other person. This is your personal work and this technique only works if it alters you and brings you closer to what you should be feeling.

When I'm coaching/teaching or directing I often need to know what your personalisation is in order to help you and be able to change it if need be. I don't recommend discussing it with the actor(s) you're playing opposite. The last thing you want them to do is to play up to your personalisation or, in the worst-case scenario, mock you.

Personalisation can not only make your connection to your character complete but can make the actors you're acting opposite better or *even* better. Supplying real love or feelings has to be a million times better than manufacturing them, right?

SUBSTITUTIONS

This is not dissimilar to personalisation. **Substitution** is finding equivalent feelings, events and situations. Often when I'm working on monologues with students, I will get them, as an exercise, to substitute names and places to something familiar and personal. For example, in *The Woolgatherer* by William Mastrosimone there's a speech about a young woman witnessing abuse to exotic birds in a zoo. She has to be really upset and affected by the assault and death of these birds. What if you like the speech but can't relate to being so personally upset about this event; intellectually it's upsetting but it's not translating in your performance. In this case I would encourage substitution. Do you have a dog, cat, horse etc. that you care about? If so, then it would be good to use them in place of the birds. Every time the birds are mentioned you should substitute the reference to the birds with your pet's name. By doing this simple exercise you should immediately feel connected, upset and angry about the situation. I sometimes like to go one step further and get you to substitute the entire situation. I will take a portion of the speech and give you an idea of what I mean.

> And one night a gang of boys came by with radios to their ears and cursing real bad, you know, F and everything. And I was, you know, ascared. And they started saying things to me, you know, dirty things, and laughing at the birds. And one kid threw a stone to see how close he could splash the birds, and then another kid tried to see how close he could splash the birds, and then they all started throwing stones *at* the birds, and I started screaming STOP IT! and a stone hit the bird's leg and it bended like a straw and the birds kneeled over in the water, flapping wings in the water, and the kids kept laughing and throwing stones and I kept screaming STOP IT! STOP IT! but they couldn't hear me through that ugly music on the radios and kept laughing and cursing and throwing stones, and I ran and get the zoo guard and he got his club and we ran to the place of the birds but the kids were gone. And there was white feathers on the water. And the water was real still. And there was big swirls of blood. And the birds were real still. Their beaks a little open. Legs broke. Toes curled. Still.

And here's a version I did with a student who told me she was very attached to her dogs. As an exercise I helped her transpose the following speech and change it accordingly.

> And one night a gang of boys came by with radios to their ears and cursing real bad, you know, F and everything. And I was, you know, ascared. And they started saying things to me, you know dirty things, and laughing *at my cute dogs Mickey and Minnie.* And one kid threw a stone to see how close he could splash *my dogs*, and then another kid *started to throw stones to splash them*, and then they started throwing stones *at my dogs* and I started screaming STOP IT! and a stone hit *Mickey's leg and it bled like a fountain and she kneeled over in the water, then she started waving her paws to keep afloat* and the kids kept laughing and throwing stones and

I kept screaming STOP IT! STOP IT! but they couldn't hear me through that ugly music on the radios and kept laughing and cursing and throwing stones, and I ran and got the zoo guard and he got his club and we ran to the *pond* but the kids were gone. *And there were clumps of fur on the water.* And the water was real still. And there was big swirls of blood. *And the dogs were floating. Their mouths a little open. Legs broke. Tails limp.* Still.

Once this has been done, it should make it impossible to be impartial. Naming your dogs should make this speech personal and connected. In this case I had to tweak the text so that it made sense but often you can just substitute names. Once you've tested that your substitution works, you should rehearse with it a few times and then go back to the original text; the connection, feeling and emotion should all be there.

ENDOWMENT

This technique is used to endow an object or person with a *quality* so that it changes *you* and not the other person or the inanimate object. **Endowment** as opposed to personalisation tends to affect/change you in a more extreme way.

For example, you might have a scene in a film where you are playing against a green screen – Computer Generated Imagery (CGI) – and you have to be afraid of a horrific creature that's not actually there. Or you have something that's been made out of cardboard and is held up on a stick to represent the creature that will be CGI'd later. This is exactly the time to endow. The green screen forces you to use your imagination: what are you most afraid of? Spiders? Cockroaches? Rats? Maybe you could endow the cardboard on a stick as a giant tarantula…? Would that be enough to elicit fear and horror in you? You can also endow the actor you're playing opposite.

Depending on what you need you could perhaps use the following to find extreme horror, repulsion or fear. You could imagine that the person you're playing opposite has bad breath (smells of vomit), is a giant cockroach, is a psychopath. If you want to find extreme arrogance you could imagine everyone around you is deaf.

Not only can you use endowment on other actors, you can use endowment on yourself. If you have to be legless drunk or perhaps a paraplegic you could imagine you are a rag doll where you have no bones at all in your body making you completely floppy. If you have to be other-worldly, say from another planet, you could imagine you are made from head to foot of delicate glass or bone china including your lips, so if you talk too fast or move too quickly you will crack. You could endow a normal chair as if it were a throne. Or a plastic cup as if it were a goblet.

I think you get the idea – endowment changes *you* and not the other actors or the inanimate objects around you. You must commit to the endowment fully otherwise it will not change you enough.

(iii) OBJECTIVES / ACTIONS

What is an **objective**? It's a want, a need, a desire, an intention, an **action** that you need to have in *every* scene you're in. I will try to lay this out as simply as possible but don't underestimate how important it is to have an objective or action. If you think about it, you're not entering into any given scene to 'play' a scene, you're there to *'want or need'* something. Your responsibility as an actor is to identify **'What do you want?'**.

The first thing you must do after you have read the script is re-read it and work out what your objective is – you need it for your through-line of the script. If you're in it from beginning to end this should be relatively clear. If you're only in it for one or two scenes or sporadically you still need to work out your overall objective. It doesn't matter how small your part is, you need to know your purpose for being in the room and what you want. Even if you have a non-speaking part or you only have dialogue in certain scenes you will still need to work out your objective/action.

1. Find your objective for the entire arc of the play or film.

2. Find your objective for each scene you're in.

Then you need to find a **scenic action/physical action or activity**. A **scenic action** is what you are physically doing in the scene – giving yourself a physical life, which is your reason for being there. Sometimes this is directorial, sometimes this is dictated by the script and often it is unscripted, therefore you should find one or several at all costs. Let's go back to real life for a minute. Have you ever seen anyone just sit in a chair like a statue listening to conversation? Or stand stock still just listening? I doubt it very much. You twiddle a pen, fiddle with your hair, doodle, scratch, bite your lip... My point is, we're always in *action* and I can't stress enough how important it is to have a life on stage or on set.

Here is a list of **scenic action/physical action/activity** ideas that you could use in rehearsal and in performance.

> Make a bed
> Set a table
> Re-arrange cushions
> Clean the room
> Polish the cutlery
> Prepare food
> Change clothes
> Apply make-up
> Polish nails
> Write a note/letter
> Read a paper
> Do a crossword puzzle
> Pack clothes in a suitcase
> Unpack clothes
> Sew a button or darn an item of clothing
> Iron
> Eat some fruit
> Take a drink

I'm not advocating you should defy your director or you should upstage your fellow actors. I'm not suggesting that for one minute. I am trying to inspire you and make sure you are not left stranded or feeling self-conscious because you have nothing to do.

Let me return to finding the overall action/objective for the play or film. After you have read the script you need to figure out what your overall objective is. This can also apply to monologues. Here are a few examples of an objective:

> To end the relationship
> To get revenge
> To get married
> To seek understanding
> To repair the relationship
> To resolve your differences

As you can see, an objective is short and concise and should not be a verbose explanation of what your intentions are – this would be 'unactable' and could be very confusing.

An objective is something you seek to attain within your journey in the play, film or monologue and it can change. If your intention is to win the girl and halfway through the play/film you get the girl, now your objective might be to elope with her. My point is you must always have an intention no matter what.

So far then you have to:

☐ Find your **objective** for the entire arc of the play or film.

☐ Find your **personal objective** for each scene you're in.

☐ Find your **scenic/physical action** in the scene.

Now you have to find your **super objective**, which is what you want in life (overall) but often will not be able to achieve right away:

> To get married
> To have children
> To buy a house
> To be famous
> To make lots of money
> To have power

Often super objectives are ambitions. You have to work this out, as it will help with the through-line and arc of your character.

Therefore:

☐   Find your **objective** for the entire arc of the play or film.

☐   Find your **objective** for each scene you're in.

☐   Find your **scenic/physical action/activity** in each scene.

☐   Find your **super objective** – ambition.

(iv) SCRIPT BREAKDOWN / MAKING CHOICES

Once you have chosen your monologue, read the play, researched and found out how you can connect to the character, you now need to tackle the text.

I don't believe that you should just perform speeches over and over again until it sounds good. You need to make choices. A lot of actors tend to rehearse speeches into the ground until it sounds right, that's the worst thing any actor could do. If you think about it, it's very cliché just to launch into the text without making any specific decisions. By this I mean, it's all too easy for an actor to put on a voice, attitude, emotion or comment on the text. This is often done subconsciously. If, for example you have done some acting and have got into some very bad habits, what's to stop you applying those habits without realizing it when you do the speech? There's a danger it could all be washed over with a banal generality. That's the last thing you or a director or audition panel want to see. I understand there's a fear of 'what if you make the wrong choice.' Well, you don't set out to make wrong choices. You can't second-guess what they're looking for, unless they give you a very specific breakdown, which is rare. In which case, it's better to make a choice than no choice. They can always be changed but you you have to make some first! This shows you've thought about the role or the monologue, you're bringing something to the table. Often directors don't know what they're looking for, in which case trying to second-guess how they might or might not see the speech or how they would want you to perform it is suicidal. You have to be brave, make specific, informed character choices, take a risk and play them fully!

I think the best way to clarify what I'm saying is to take a sample speech and break it down into informed choices.

The Typists

By Murray Schisgal

My family never had money problems. In that respect we were very fortunate. My father made a good living, while he was alive, that is. He passed away when I was seventeen. You could say he and my mother had a fairly happy marriage. At least we never knew when they were angry with one another, and that's a good thing for children. I have a sister. Charlotte. She's older than I am. She's married now and we don't bother much with each other. But when we were younger you wouldn't believe what went on. Every time we quarrelled, according to my parents she was right; I was always wrong. She got everything she wanted, no matter what, and I had to be content with the leftovers. It was just unbearable. Anyway, my father was sick for a long time before he passed away. He had this ring, it was a beautiful ring, with a large onyx stone in it, and when I was a girl I used to play with it. I'd close one eye and I'd look inside of it and I'd see hundreds and hundreds of beautiful red and blue stars. My father had always promised me that ring; he always said it belonged to me. I thought for certain he'd give it to me before he passed away, but he didn't say anything about it; not a word. Well, afterward, I saw it. You know where I saw it? On my sister's finger. He had given it to her. Now I don't think that's a background that leaves many possibilities for development. I don't forgive my father; definitely not. And I don't forgive my sister. My mother, whom I now support with my hard work, still says I'm wrong.

I guess the biggest pitfall of anyone sight-reading a monologue for the first time, is to read it in a very rushed and emotional way, over-emphasizing certain words, using an upward inflection on the ends of some sentences and exhaling some breath at the beginning of others, making the character sound very breathy, almost like a faint laugh. In other words, there is a tendency to make the character untruthful.

I would like to show you that applying some simple technique to the speech will make all the difference, it will make it more truthful. This could be called '**table work**', in other words technical work on the text; once you've done it, this will free you up so you will have a clear through-line as to what your character is saying, especially once you work out the action or objective of the speech.

One of the first questions you have to ask yourself is

1. 'What do you think the main purpose of the speech is?'

Once you ascertain it's about how Sylvia feels about her family, you then have to figure out:

2. What is your objective?

You have to figure out the action of the speech. Not the description of the story i.e. how Sylvia feels about her family or about how unhappy she is about the ring that her father gave to her sister – that is the situation.

The question you need to ask yourself is '**What reaction do you want from the other person?**' The trap is to think 'What am I telling him?'. Telling is not very creative and certainly isn't a choice. It's a given that most speeches are about someone telling or saying or asking but in terms of finding a through-line this is the wrong way to go about it.

In this instance the objective of the speech is to get understanding. The objective shouldn't be complicated even though it might seem complex to get to it. Once you have found the objective, you can write that on top of the speech in pencil, not pen, as you might want to change it down the line. It should read like a headline or heading.

To Get Understanding

This should now guide you in a much more specific way, if you think '**What do I want?**'. If you refer back to my Stanislavski's 10 Questions in CHAPTER 5 you will find this as question number 5: **Objectives – 'What do I want?'**.

So now you have to break the speech down into beats/units. Think of this as the musical score/notes for actors! Breaking down the text is like 'scoring' your text.

OK, so the next phase is to try and find the first beat and put a transitive/active verb on to it. You need to find out the subtext, the psychology of what you're saying. In other words, what do you want to make the other person feel? What do you have to do to affect the other person? These become your choices, your character choices. This gives what you do nuance and colour.

Let's take the first beat. A new **beat** starts every time you have a new thought and go on to talk about something different. Sometimes this is not always easy to identify but the more choices you can find the more varied the speech will be. Unless you're breaking down a scene that consists of one-liners, in which you will need to find a transitive/active verb for each line, in most instances concerning monologues, you should break the speech into chunks/beats and find a verb for each one. There are some practitioners that believe you should find a verb for each line. Not only is this difficult but almost impossible to 'play' and even harder to learn. Most people don't change their **thought/activity** on every sentence; it usually takes a few sentences in order to make someone feel something.

OK, let's attempt to find the first verb.

The Typists

My family never had money problems. In that respect we were very fortunate. My father made a good living, while he was alive, that is. He passed away when I was seventeen. You could say he and my mother had a fairly happy marriage. At least we never knew when they were angry with one another, and that's a good thing for children. I have a sister. Charlotte. She's older than I am. She's married now and we don't bother much with each other.

I would say the first beat stops here as you then go on to talk about when you were younger. Now you have to ask yourself **'What is the**

character doing here?' Careful not to fall into the trap of saying 'Talking about my family' or 'Explaining' etc. Briefly analyse this section. What are you doing? You're talking about your family and parents' marriage, about how you grew up etc. Therefore, you're sharing. You need to write the verb in the margin and draw a line where the verb ends.

To Share

Let's go on to the next beat.

> But when we were younger you wouldn't believe what went on. Every time we quarrelled, according to my parents she was right; I was always wrong. She got everything she wanted, no matter what, and I had to be content with the leftovers. It was just unbearable.

What are you doing here? You're talking badly about your sister... But you need to think what's behind what you're saying. So instead of 'talking' or 'explaining' you might want to go with 'complaining' as that's what Sylvia is doing in this section.

To Complain

OK, hopefully this is getting a little easier. I'm leading you to try to find the verbs, otherwise, if I give them to you, you'll be dependent on me and will never learn how to get there yourself. I must also tell you that it can take awhile for actors to learn this technique. But I assure you, the more texts you break down the easier it gets. Don't forget these are just choices, character choices that the actor must be able to decipher. These are not definitive, which is why I'm encouraging you to mark up in pencil because down the line if you think of a better, more succinct choice that works for you, you should use it, providing it fits.

Often I'm working with international actors, for whom English is their second language. If, for example, I suggest the verb they use is TO BELITTLE and they don't know what that word means, I need to use a synonym that resonates with them like TO PATRONISE or TO PUT DOWN. You have to find a verb that you understand...if you don't understand the word how will you know how to play it?

OK let's look at the next beat.

> Anyway, my father was sick for a long time before he passed
> away. He had this ring, it was a beautiful ring, with a large
> onyx stone in it, and when I was a girl I used to play with it.

You might think the verb in this instance is TO GET SYMPATHY. Not far off at all, to be even more specific I think the verb is TO GET EMPATHY. Empathy is a mixture of sympathy and understanding so I think this verb is better.

Let's go on to the next section.

> I'd close one eye and I'd look inside of it and I'd see hundreds
> and hundreds of beautiful red and blue stars.

I know it seems like Sylvia is describing the colours of the ring, but you have to remember most of the verbs you choose should be to affect the other person.

There are exceptions and you can have verbs to yourself – for example, I think this beat is **To Reminisce.** As long as you have an **activity** to yourself, that means you're in action and not just playing the problem, mood, condition, emotion etc. Examples of activities to yourself could be: to reflect, to ponder, to contemplate, to mull over etc.

Onto the next beat.

> My father had always promised me that ring; he always said
> it belonged to me. I thought for certain he'd give it to me
> before he passed away, but he didn't say anything about it;
> not a word.

You should've got **To Get Sympathy** – I think Sylvia is clearly vying for it.

OK let's go onto the next beat.

> Well, afterward, I saw it. You know where I saw it? On my
> sister's finger. He had given it to her.

You could say Sylvia's getting angry here but be careful because that's an emotion. You could also say she's trying to get a reaction but the next question you should ask yourself is, 'She's trying to get a reaction, how, by doing what?' By trying **To Shock** would be the right answer.

I guess I'm making it seem so easy, well, in a way it is but it's difficult in its simplicity. I think the danger is, as I said before, that everyone wants to make emotional choices and they're just not proactive and therefore don't serve the text or the character. Don't forget it's also experience that I have under my belt. After many years of applying this technique, it becomes second-nature and you start thinking and using verbs in your own everyday life. For example, when a friend really wants something from you and they are all of a sudden sweet and overfriendly, you could say they were trying TO CHARM or TO ENDEAR you. Kids are the perfect example of how you should play these activities. Next time you're around any small kids just watch how they play very clear verbs instinctively, like TO WEAR DOWN, TO OVERWHELM, TO PLEAD, TO MELT.

Let's tackle the last beat.

> Now I don't think that's a background that leaves many possibilities for development. I don't forgive my father; definitely not. And I don't forgive my sister. My mother, whom I now support with my hard work, still says I'm wrong.

Sylvia is being quite defiant here, which makes the verb – To what?
To Defend
So the speech should now look like this.

Objective
To Get Understanding

> My family never had money problems. In that respect we were very fortunate. My father made a good living, while he was alive, that is. He passed away when I was seventeen. You could say he and my mother had a fairly happy marriage. At least we never knew when they were angry with one another, and that's a good thing for children. I have a sister. Charlotte. She's older than I am. She's married now and we don't bother much with each other. **To Share**

But when we were younger you wouldn't believe what went on. Every time we quarrelled, according to my parents she was right; I was always wrong. She got everything she wanted, no matter what, and I had to be content with the leftovers. It was just unbearable. TO COMPLAIN

Anyway, my father was sick for a long time before he passed away. He had this ring, it was a beautiful ring, with a large onyx stone in it, and when I was a girl I used to play with it. TO GET EMPATHY

I'd close one eye and I'd look inside of it and I'd see hundreds and hundreds of beautiful red and blue stars. TO REMINISCE

My father had always promised me that ring; he always said it belonged to me. I thought for certain he'd give it to me before he passed away, but he didn't say anything about it; not a word. TO GET SYMPATHY

Well, afterward, I saw it. You know where I saw it? On my sister's finger. He had given it to her. TO SHOCK

Now I don't think that's a background that leaves many possibilities for development. I don't forgive my father; definitely not. And I don't forgive my sister. My mother, whom I now support with my hard work, still says I'm wrong. TO DEFEND

It would now be interesting for you to read the text aloud, whether you're male or female. This could just be a good exercise in practising how to apply **transitive/active verbs**. So as you read each beat, you must 'play' the verb fully as you're reading it.

Just to reiterate, what I have just done is not an academic exercise. I've done this in order to give you a practical and organic way to say the lines. Therefore if the verbs remain static on the page and you don't do anything with them, this means what I've done just now is theoretical, not practical, therefore virtually useless.

A helpful tip from an actor I trained (who is also dyslexic): he uses a different colour highlighter for each verb, so he can clearly see the verb changes. I think this is a great way to mark up your script, so I would suggest you try this method and see if it helps.

Your choices should always be proactive and never static. Therefore, you want to avoid making choices like:

To Listen
To Say
To Tell
To Ask
To Inform

Before you start this exercise, remember, there's no point having the verbs in the margin unless you 'play' them fully. So if the verb is 'To Share' really share – you can't 'share' with someone in voice only. 'To Complain' – really complain and the same with 'Getting Empathy'. That also means playing the **physical action** of the verb.

Have a look at the appendix for a list of tangible and visceral **transitive/active verbs** that are very active and in some cases easier to use.

In the next chapter I will take some verbs one by one, beat by beat and we'll focus on how you play verbs in order to affect the other person.

I will also talk you through how you can rehearse this at home once you have found your substitutions and personalisations.

(v) SENSE MEMORY / AFFECTIVE / EMOTIONAL MEMORY

It's important that as an actor you're able to dig deep and access the feeling, emotion or memory that's needed for the scene. It's not always a given that these personal memories will be at the forefront of your mind, therefore these exercises are there for you to use when you need to access something specific for your character. These personal memories shouldn't be visible on stage or screen, they should merely manifest at the point in the scene when you need to break down and cry or shudder with embarrassment or laugh hysterically. Even if you are able to do this spontaneously, I doubt very much you'll be able to do it on cue or for every 'take' or sustain this every night in every performance. This is where technique kicks in and I will now break down the stages you need to go through as homework in order for it to seem effortless in performance.

SENSE MEMORY

This is being able to recall a sensory memory that you might need in a scene. It could be anything from recalling the strong taste of bourbon to the breathtaking sea cliff views. **Sense memory** involves the 5 senses: sight, sound, taste, smell, touch.

Can you remember that time you winced at the sharp taste of an alcoholic spirit? Or got nostalgic from the smell of salty sea air, romantic at the sound of the crashing waves, weepy at the sight of your childhood home? What sights, sounds, smells, touch and taste can you instantly recall? As actors you are required to feel hot, cold, tired, sick, drunk, shocked, hurt etc. etc. Often on stage and on film sets you are not experiencing what you're meant to experience. You might have to look like you're freezing cold and instead it's boiling hot on stage and even hotter under the film set lights. When you have to be asleep in bed and wake up in the middle of a scene. Undoubtedly your substitutes for alcohol such as whiskey, rum, brandy, gin and vodka will be cold tea/apple juice and water.

It's your job as an actor to make whatever you're doing believable, therefore you better locate exactly where and how you're meant to be feeling beforehand; general hot, cold, tired, unwell or drunk acting can look very cliché. Nobody feels generally unwell, pain is usually localized. Is it a sharp pain on the left or right side of your abdomen? Is it a dull or stabbing pain? Is it in your belly area? Cramp-like pain? Indigestion? Bloated with gas? Does that mean you have to sit or lie in a certain position to ease the pain? How do you cope with the pain in company? I'm sure you deal with it differently than when you're by yourself i.e. letting it all hang out... What happens when you can't indulge in your condition? Does it mean you fold your arms around your abdomen to ease your discomfort and by doing this hide the pain you're suffering?

If you're not entirely sure how you feel and react why don't you observe yourself the next time you have a stomach ache and really pinpoint where the actual pain is and what you do to relieve it and how you cope in company when you can't indulge in the pain? The same goes for headaches and migraine. Do you feel dull pain over one eye? Or pressure over your entire forehead? Or is it a throbbing pain at the top of your head? How does the pain manifest in your behaviour? When you want to experience the localized pain, close your eyes and try to pinpoint and recall the exact pain you want to experience and don't be surprised if the pain you are trying to evoke appears for a while. Of course you can also do this with conditions i.e. feeling tired, sweating and shivering cold.

Scenes with characters feeling hung over, drunk or tipsy crop up quite a bit and I always think it's very dodgy when an actor sets out to 'play drunk'. Most people in real life who get drunk feel embarrassed that they are slurring their words or walking unsteadily. Therefore why would actors do it when playing drunk? The best way to deal with this situation and do it truthfully is to find your drunken state and play against it; i.e. play sober, which I assure you is much more interesting to perform and to watch. For example, if you get tipsy at a dinner party I'm sure you wouldn't want to make this obvious to the person you're talking to and would do everything you can to mask slurring your words and try to walk straight. In other words you desperately cling on to self-restraint as much as possible rather than flaunt your uncontrolled self.

What if you've never drunk alcohol or been drunk? Well, I'm not suggesting that you go out and get drunk but I do suggest you smell the exact alcohol you are meant to be drinking in the play or film. Whether it's a Merlot (red wine) or Chardonnay (white wine), Budweiser, tequila, rum or whiskey. Each of these drinks has its own particular smell and will certainly give you an idea of the strength of taste as well as the character of the drink. If you do drink, I'm not advocating that you go out and get drunk on the two bottles of Jack Daniels your character craves. But you might want to sample your character's favourite drink... You might not have tasted a Tequila Sunrise or a dry Martini before or you may not remember what they taste like. However, most people who drink usually have experienced what it feels like to get drunk, at least once. If this is the case, you should also be able to remember how you felt. If not, I suggest you close your eyes and do a **sense memory** exercise to pinpoint the exact taste and smell. You can also apply this to how it feels to be hung over.

There's an instant physical exercise I give actors to help them access feeling drunk (without getting drunk). This has to be done under supervision as it could potentially be dangerous. One of the main sensory memories of being drunk is dizziness. Right before a scene or an improvisation I get the actor(s) who are meant to be inebriated to spin around until they get very light-headed. In order to do this you need to have people around spotting/protecting them and making sure the actor(s) do not get hurt or crash into anything. If you need to be legless drunk then I recommend intense spinning to be done immediately prior to your entrance. If you have to crash into furniture and be out of control, I guarantee that you will find it from doing this alone. If the sense memory/feeling you're trying to accomplish is one of disorientation and dizziness, I recommend that you spin about five minutes prior to your scene and have a few seconds/minute before you make your entrance. This physical preparation will no doubt give you the sense memory of drunkenness.

AFFECTIVE MEMORY

This is a memory of something that has affected you. This could be anything from reading an email with some upsetting news, to receiving a text from your boyfriend who's splitting up with you, to getting up in the morning and discovering you have no coffee, to leaving your house and discovering you can't find your keys or mobile phone, to tripping down the escalators in a shopping mall or spilling a drink over new clothes. What happens when you play a character that has to get annoyed about something or feel embarrassed, ashamed or guilty? Well, you need to access memories in your own life that have affected you and then you'll be able to use them on stage or on set.

Affective memory should transport you from one state of being to another. For example, you start your day as usual and are feeling alright until the phone rings and you get some bad news, you didn't land that job – this plummets you into a very bad mood. Or you receive an email saying that your sister, while travelling abroad, was involved in a car crash and you burst out crying. The news you hear completely changes your mood and feeling. Or you could be quietly watching TV at home and your best friend comes in with a ridiculous outfit and you burst into complete hysterics.

To find your affective memory you need to be in a place of relaxation. Therefore once you decide on what you're trying to recall – sadness, laughter, guilt, humiliation, nerves etc. – you should then think of the event you want to recall and follow the relaxation exercise below.

Once you're relaxed, close your eyes and imagine a film screen and go back to your first memory of the day in question. If the incident you're trying to remember happened in the middle of the day your recall should start from the first moments of the day when you were feeling alright.

Let's take an example of something your character experiences but you have not in real life. What if your character is supposed to feel ashamed of her body and doesn't want to put on her wedding dress but in real life you don't have an issue with your body so your character's dilemma isn't a problem? You still need to feel ashamed – it's your responsibility as an actor to get under the character's skin and be connected. You're going to have to find another memory where you *have* felt ashamed. You can go as far back as you need to as long as whatever you recall makes *you* feel ashamed. I don't mean in an intellectual way, as that can't help you, but if the memory actively makes you feel ashamed at the moment of recall then that's the one you should use.

EMOTIONAL MEMORY

This is more extreme than affective memory as it's a memory which has to be emotional, has to recreate a shattering and traumatic event in your life.

The distance from this enormous emotional situation must *not* be less than 5 years. This is in order for you to have sufficient detachment and recovery from the event to be able to control it for creative purposes.

This exercise centres on 4 major emotions:

Extreme anger – Laughter – Tears – Fear

When you've gone into your past and selected an event, you must relax completely by lying down and following the exercise below. Once you are fully loosened up, close your eyes and try to recall (either silently or out loud to yourself or to someone who's physically there) through your 5 senses what you saw, heard, smelled, tasted and touched. You must start at the beginning of the experience and go through every detail that is possible to remember. It might surprise you how much you remember when you put yourself back inside the event. If you stay relaxed and don't push for any result, you'll find that a sight, sound, taste, smell or touch will trigger off the emotion and you'll be laughing or crying etc. as fully as when it originally happened – only now, because of the time gap, you will be able to control it. I suggest you repeat this exercise a few more times within a few weeks to secure your trigger. Once you feel it's there, you're ready to transfer your trigger to any scene in a play or film.

TRIGGERS

Once you have established your **trigger** for your affective or emotional memory you have to then test it in rehearsals or at home to see how early on in the scene you need to place it to make you cry. You might need to place the trigger exactly on the line you say 'I'm sorry dad I never meant to hurt you'. If that's the case, you need to put the trigger on any word in that sentence. If you're meant to break down halfway through the scene you might want to put your trigger at the top of the scene and slowly let it take effect, so it's fully there by the time you have to cry. A lot of this is trial and error and it might take a few rehearsals at home before you work out how long you need for your trigger to take effect.

The same principle can be used with finding a song that makes you laugh or feel agitated, angry etc. Please refer to CHAPTER 7.

Usually triggers are strong and instant but sometimes you have to allow more time for the trigger to work. If you need it on a certain line and you're only getting it if you place the trigger a page earlier, then it might not be strong enough. However, you could place it a page earlier to make yourself feel vulnerable and then find another trigger for the exact line you have your meltdown on.

Relaxation

Find a nice quiet spot to lie down and close your eyes –

Scrunch your toes – hold 2, 3, 4 – release 5, 6, 7.

Contract your calves – hold 2, 3, 4 – release 5, 6, 7.

Clench your thighs – hold 2, 3, 4 – release 5, 6, 7.

Pull in your buttocks – hold 2, 3, 4 – release 5, 6, 7.

Contract your torso – hold 2, 3, 4 – release 5, 6, 7.

Clench your fists and pull up your shoulders to your ears – hold 2,3, 4 – release 5, 6, 7.

Scrunch your face – hold 2,3,4 – release 5,6,7.

Now you are going to tighten, tighten and hold all of the above

2, 3, 4, 5.

Then slowly release starting with toes then calves, thighs, buttocks, torso, shoulders, arms, fists then face.

Repeat.

You should feel all the stress disappearing after the slow release. If you still feel tense, repeat the exercise.

7. CHARACTER PREPARATION

So you have an important audition coming up – professional or drama school entry – and obviously you want to do as well as you possibly can. Or maybe you have the lead in a feature film or a great part in a play but you keep hitting a stumbling block when practising at home or in rehearsals. Why do you find something once or twice but then it keeps running away from you? Why can't you find a consistency with your performance? Once you've done all the searching, backstory, text work, you might be at a stage where the play is blocked and you're off book...ready to shoot your scene, or just ready to rehearse your monologue or role – It's no wonder you can't sustain your performance if you don't do any character preparation!

Now by character prep I'm not talking about a voice or physical warm-up. That's something different that should be done prior to rehearsals or performance. (If you're lucky enough to be in a big company like the National or RSC you will have the privilege of doing company warm-ups.) I'm talking about specific, detailed character preparation, which will springboard you into the heart and soul of the character. I work with actors who come to me to work on their sides or monologues and, without fail, just want to launch into it. It's no surprise that what they're doing isn't very wondrous, after about the fifth or sixth time they start hitting their stride and I would say by the end it's really quite good. OK now, that's not great is it...? How many shots do you usually have in an audition? How many takes would you really feel comfortable doing when everyone's waiting for you to nail it pretty much in the first take? Do you see a pattern forming here...? This is where I believe character preparation is crucial. This is an immediate preparation that should be done prior to a big scene/take or audition.

There are 3 categories to preparation:

Objects
Music
Physical

OBJECTS

Here are some examples of how you can use **objects** to springboard you into the speech/scene feeling connected. Of course all these have to be rehearsed and tested to know if it's the right prep.

What if your speech or scene was based around feeling bad about something that someone had done to you or something you had done to them. Or you have to laugh or get agitated or upset halfway through, in which case you might be able to use:

Letters/Cards

A letter from an estranged parent that you kept from when you were a teenager when things were good and you know every time you read it you're affected by it.

A letter from your boyfriend/girlfriend breaking up with you.

A card you received from your best friend that always makes you laugh.

A rejection letter

A letter of acceptance

A Will and Testament

A love letter

Jewellery

That can make you feel sentimental, happy, romantic.

Tangled-up Jewellery

That makes you feel frustrated and tormented.

Puzzles

That make you feel impatient and irritated.

These are just a few examples of how you can use objects to affect you. If you have a good sense that a specific object could make you feel a specific way, you need to test that object by reading that letter, at first silently then out loud. Try to untangle that necklace or solve that puzzle. This could take anywhere from 5-20 minutes to have an effect.

This is not an intellectual exercise so it's not about the 'idea' of the letter or forcing it to have the same effect it did two years ago. If you try it and the letter feels meaningless to you now or you feel numb or untouched by it, then you know it's not right. If on the other hand it starts to work, good, allow the tears, sadness or frustration or whatever you're working for to manifest then go straight into your speech. This is a great start. However, it might've taken you 20 minutes to get to that point, which is not very practical every time you need to rehearse the speech or scene, and what about at the audition, performance or filming, what happens then?

Well, first you need to make sure that the object you used was not a one-off. So, a few hours later or the next day when you're in a different mindset, try using it again in exactly the same way. If it works again, bravo, you found your object.

Now we go onto the next stage, which is:

FINDING YOUR TRIGGER

Obviously you can't go through that process every single time. So now you have to work out what part of the letter moved you to feeling hurt, angry, betrayed, bitter? What sentence triggered off your feelings? Or was it the 'P.S' bit at the end of the letter? Was it the hand-drawn heart that made you feel sentimental? That one bit of the puzzle that you just couldn't do?

Once you work out what your **trigger** is you barely need to use the object anymore you just think of the trigger and that should springboard you right into the heart of what you need to feel. Something that took you initially 20 minutes to find, now only takes seconds and you're right in there.

Time put aside in finding the right preparation and trigger can save you hours and hours of gruelling rehearsal until you're warmed up. After many times of testing the preparation and feeling satisfied, you can be sure that if you use it, you can hit it first time every time!

MUSIC

Finding the right song to catapult you into the heart of the scene or speech can be invaluable. It can also get you into the right zone from cold. I encourage this preparation the most. You can always tell a 'Dee' trained actor when you see someone listening to music on their iPod before a scene in a play or film.

You should be looking for a song that connects you to the bosom of the scene or feeling. If the scene or speech is period you don't have to find a song from that era. The song you choose can be from any genre as long as it is specifically chosen and tested to make you feel…what? Vulnerable, childlike, hurt, melancholic, bold, formal?

Again, you might have to listen to your chosen song at length to begin with but once you're certain it's the right song that produces the desired feeling or emotion every time, the length of your listening should decrease. Find your trigger – work out what bit of the song is triggering your feeling…? Is it the bit where the violins soar? Where the key changes? Where the second verse starts? The chorus bit? The guitar solo? The bit where his voice quivers? Once identified you really don't have to listen to the song continuously. You should get to the point where you barely have to listen to it. You could just hear it in your head or hum the trigger bit and boom you should be right in there.

This is particularly apposite when you want to use music to bring up emotion but the emotion doesn't arise till halfway through the speech or scene. Then what? You can't run off and listen to your iPod but you can plant the trigger a few lines before you need to react or cry or on an actual line.

You can rehearse triggers. Once you find a song that works and you know exactly what your trigger is, you can test it randomly when you're not in rehearsal. When you're watching TV, or driving your car, on the bus or the tube. I highly recommend that you test your triggers out of context and that way you can really judge if they're foolproof outside of a conducive environment. Randomly laughing or crying in a public place could be quite interesting indeed!

PHYSICAL PREPARATION

This can be so effective, in so many different ways. Often I get actors to use physical prep if I think they just need to loosen up. Star jumps, running up the stairs and press-ups can be highly powerful not to say exhausting, but that's the point, a lot can manifest out of exhaustion. I wouldn't necessarily recommend this before a performance, unless of course you need to run on exhausted. Undoubtedly you will have lines and there's not much point if you're so breathless that you are inaudible and no one can understand you.

Focus on using this kind of physical prep in rehearsal to free you up, make you more spontaneous. We have such a thing as muscle memory – the body remembers – so after you've done this a number of times, you will only need to do a fraction of physical prep beforehand; the body remembers what it felt like to be free and spontaneous and this in turn frees up your scene or speech.

ANIMAL WORK

There are many wonderful reasons for using 'animals' in rehearsals. I will lay out some of the functions and benefits.

If you want to find release, spontaneity, playful and childlike qualities then you should choose specific animals that lend themselves to being just that: chimpanzees, puppy dogs and kittens. The premise is that you should physically embody the animal, which means you can't do it unless you go down on all fours. You also can't be the animal unless you vocalise that dog, cat or chimp. You are not trying to 'represent', you're trying to 'be'. The only way you're going to do that, is to lose yourself in the animal. The only way you'll be able to do that is to be very physical, active and of course playful. You can give yourself the objective of finding a playmate (if there's more than one of you doing this exercise), of looking for food, of having fun, of causing havoc. The idea is that you become this animal for at least 20 minutes, continuous, without resting. You must keep moving and not break out of it. You should be feeling extremely exhausted – that's the point. The idea is to throw you off your own physical centre so after the 20 minutes or so (I have been known to keep animals going for half an hour depending on the fitness level of the actors doing it) you can go right into an improvisation, your scene or monologue. I can assure you, if this exercise is done right, you will find an amazing freedom you never had before and this can lead to all sorts of new and exciting impulses. After a while the exhilaration of the animal wears off but you should retain the new-found freedom and enjoyment that comes with this exercise.

The other use of animal work is **physical transformation**. You use this if you want to transform your physicality to explore overriding characteristics such as intense (hawk), quirky (penguin), uncouth (pig), timid (mouse), sensual (tiger), feisty (kangaroo), earthy (bear). This doesn't work using insects or birds that are mainly reliant on their wings for flying or for fish and amphibians that generally live in water. The same instructions should be used again to totally immerse yourself in the animals in order to throw you off your own physical centre. Once you have been that animal for up to half an hour you should feel physically different i.e. bear-like, tiger-like and should go straight into an improvisation, rehearsal, scene or speech so as to reap the benefits of this new-found physicality. You will know if you've done the exercise right because you should feel physically transformed and not on your centre.

PHYSICAL ESSENCE

If you just want to explore finding the essence of the animal, there's no need to transform, therefore you should do the above exercise for only 10 minutes or so. This time you don't have to feel exhausted, as you're not trying to find a different physical centre. You should just be left feeling 'horse-like' or 'chicken-like'; it is the essence you're after not the transformation. I must point out that exploring animal essence is really finding the trait of the animal; therefore you need to work out beforehand what qualities various animals represent. You don't need to study the animals in depth unless you're doing a project on them. You should of course try to observe the animal you have chosen well enough to know how it looks, sounds, moves and behaves. We should not be able to see this animal on stage or screen. The exercise is there to help you find the quality for your character.

8. HOW TO REHEARSE

So you have done all the work on your script and now you have to commit the text to memory, so you run the lines over and over and over again in the hope they will stick and soon you will have them locked in, intonation and all. Bravo, you have unwittingly side-stepped all the good work you've done on the background, character and text and now you're entering into a zone of amateur banality by rehearsing the lines into the ground so they become completely meaningless. I can't stress enough how superficial and misguided this is and how this breeds bad external habits that won't get you very far at all. However, if you have a very short time to learn lines this would be the time to learn them mechanically and put in the internal work later – working from the outside in, instead of the inside out.

Saying 'I've always learnt my lines like this' doesn't make it right. I'm not just referring to amateurs and beginners, I'm also referring to some professional actors who have developed the bad habit of learning lines by rote. There's nothing more disheartening for me than working with someone who comes for coaching with a role already learnt and when I try to suggest another way of playing their line by giving them a psychological intention, i.e. a transitive/active verb, they always say the line in exactly the same fashion as they originally did, often with nothing (no intention) behind it. They're just saying the line. When I point this out they try and take the line – let's say the line is 'I'm sorry to hear you've been feeling unwell today, can I make you some tea?' – and practise intoning it in various different ways. 'Should I say the line more like this?' Then making the inflection go down on 'sorry' and rising up on 'unwell today' and going up again on 'tea'. Then playing around with the different variants in the hope of it sounding convincing. Out of desperation they usually ask me to say the line for them – to hear how it should sound. Oh dear, the last thing I would ever, ever do is give a line reading. That defeats the whole object. It's not about how the line should sound, it's about what's behind the line and what you want to make the person feel? Which brings me nicely back to the transitive/active verbs. These verbs will be your key to learning lines. Therefore you not only have to learn the lines but also the intention behind them.

I have known many actors in the past who think breaking down their text and learning are two different entities altogether. Think again – you can't do one without the other. You should consider them synonymous with each other; you should learn your script, monologue and sides beat by beat by beat.

PHYSICAL ACTION

Each verb has to have a **physical action** in order to reach the other person. Therefore the physical action of let's say **To Scold** is not passive and therefore we have to understand that to scold someone is usually bold, direct, fairly confrontational and is rarely done sitting down. It often involves wagging or pointing a finger.

We naturally physicalise our actions in life; the **psychological action** follows a **physical action**. Let's take an obvious example of this. If the verb is TO COMFORT, we would rarely console someone just verbally, this is often followed by a physical action of holding, hugging, stroking, touching or patting. Even if no one is there when you're doing a monologue, we still have to get a sense of someone being there by how you use yourself physically.

Let's go back to *The Typists* monologue and extract the first two beats as examples. The first beat is **To Share**; when you rehearse this speech you should not go any further than the first verb. Rehearse that – remind yourself again who you are talking to and focus on how to share and what your body is doing physically. You can't share if you're sitting back or with your arms crossed, this would be the wrong **physical action**. You should not think for one second *how* you should say the lines, instead you should be focused on what are you doing to the other person (even if invisible), and in this case it's *sharing*.

The second beat is **To Complain**. The same again – You should focus on how you're complaining and be careful not to generalise. You should try and be as specific as you can on all the verbs. What are you complaining about? And to who...?

You should do this systematically for the whole speech or script – focusing on the verbs and nothing else. Once you have done this a few times you'll see that because you have concentrated on the verbs, the lines will be associated with that intention and will be learnt by default, therefore you have not just learnt the line but the intention behind the line which is the subtext.

This also leaves you free to be directed. If I wanted to change what you were doing, it wouldn't be a case of altering the rendition of the line, but adjusting your intention and because you didn't lock in a fixed pattern/way of saying the line, this shouldn't throw you at all.

Often when I'm coaching or rehearsing I can't go very far if the actors don't know how to play the physical action. Sometimes it's easier when you don't have the words to hide behind or to bounce off. Frequently I isolate the verb and just get the actors to find their physicality and the specificity of the verb – hence the subtext. You have to understand the verb to play the verb.

Often when I do workshops abroad the actors are working in their own language. Everyone is amazed I can critique the actors when I don't understand what they're saying, including the actors I'm critiquing. This is because sometimes the words get in the way and actors can hide behind them; take the words away and what are you left with? Physical and psychological intentions – actions speak louder than words!

Let's look at some verbs:

How do you intimidate someone?
Well intimidation is close to threatening but they are different. Threatening is more direct and 'in your face' whereas intimidation is more menacing and has the quality of inpredictability. So if you're intimidating someone you're often towering over them or standing behind them or even walking slowly around them. Your status has to be higher than theirs.

How do you guilt-trip someone?
Guilt is psychological and often indirect. You'll never be able to properly guilt-trip someone if it's too forthright as it will tip into accusing them or hurting them. Guilt-tripping is making a person feel bad psychologically; in this instance words quite often become redundant and it's the physical action of turning

or walking away or even leaving the room that can really have the desired effect. The silent treatment works a dream too.

How do you overwhelm someone?

You can overwhelm someone with news but this has to be pretty specific as you can tip into shocking, which is something else. A strong physical presence can overwhelm someone – if you jump on them or show them a lot of love/affection by hugging them and flooding them with presents, flowers, chocolates. This can tip into being overbearing and overpowering so you need to be very specific.

Take a risk.

You mustn't be afraid to take risks. By this I mean if you have worked out your **objectives** and **transitive/active verbs**, you shouldn't play it safe and sit on the fence, so to speak, and play your intention so small that 'What you want' is not clear at all. Once you have made your choices you should have the confidence to play them fully otherwise they will remain on paper or in your head and will render what you do boring because no one will be able to see your 'want' or what you are doing to the other person.

Instead of getting into a rut rehearsing your lines over and over and over again, concentrate on not just playing the verbs, but making sure you play them fully. The same goes if you're rehearsing opposite another character; instead of rehearsing your scene for the umpteenth time, focus on whether you're affecting the other character. Are you 'Getting his Empathy' enough…? Ask him, 'Did I affect you?'. If the answer is 'No, not really', rehearse again till you are getting his empathy. This will force you to gear change and play the verb more fully, physicalise and commit to it. The same goes for his next beat and so on and so forth. You should try to be honest with each other and say if you're being affected enough. The aim is to get it to a point where you have to listen, to receive, which leaves you open and very much in the moment. Moment-to-moment acting is what you should be striving for.

If you're not in a position where you can rehearse this way with your fellow actor(s) you just have to learn to be your own judge as to whether or not you're playing the verbs fully enough. Don't ever expect other actors to go along with you – if they do it's a bonus. I can assure you, if I were watching a scene and you were playing your intentions and the other actor wasn't, it will be markedly clear who's the superior, connected and more interesting actor. Don't ever dumb down just because other actors don't work this way or even dare to trash it. It's often because they don't understand it and it's easier to undermine it than to step up to the plate and try to be a better actor.

SURVIVING A LONG RUN IN A SHOW OR A TOUR

It's so easy to go into autopilot mode or coast a performance when you've been in a show for a long time. I believe this is your golden opportunity to perfect your craft. If you stop listening you stop receiving what the other actors are giving you; even worse if the other actors stop listening too and just react mechanically to everything. Sometimes you lock in a performance that you found in the first few weeks of the run; it worked, the audience reactions were good and you picked up rave reviews. I'm not sure that anyone sets out to freeze a performance, sometimes it's inexperience, sometimes it's insecurity and sometimes it gradually happens without you realizing.

You need to be cognisant of the fact that there's a real danger of this occurring right from the get-go. Therefore you need to take certain measures so that the moment complacency starts creeping into your performance you become aware of it. You can stop this happening by acknowledging that it's a perfect opportunity to allow your character to grow, breathe and develop, and the only way this is going to happen is if you are using the technique.

If another actor decides to play a different transitive/active verb on you and you react in the same way you've always reacted every night, that means you've stopped listening and are not in the moment. If you want to keep your performance fresh and alive as opposed to stagnant and stale, you have to actively play clear, strong objectives and listen, ready to receive what's being played back at you. This is real acting and reacting – moment-to-moment acting – and I guarantee you every night will be consistently slightly different and fresh.

I recently worked with the very accomplished singer Ramin Karimloo in *Love Never Dies* in the West End. He was playing the same character of The Phantom he had played in *The Phantom of the Opera* for the past three years and had just signed a new contract for the sequel. He realised that there was a real danger of not working to his full potential and wanted to make the most out of playing the same character but ten years on. Knowing that you've got at least a two-year run, there's every danger that you will coast. He asked me to coach him on the role so he could also apply a technique he had never used before to The Phantom. However well you think you might know your character there's always room to develop and it's not a given that you know what choices to make on the lines. It might surprise some people to know that this technique does apply itself very nicely to libretti and in this case all the dialogue was sung.

We ended up breaking down all the beats in the score, which gave him the fantastic opportunity of applying the new choices we had made in increments every night, which in turn gave his character more depth, kept it psychological and fresh. It also upped the ante for the other actors around him as The Phantom was not playing the scenes quite in the same way as he was previously. This in no way meant he was defying direction or trying to upstage the other actors. On the contrary, this just meant specific choices had now been made alongside decisions on inner conflict (**obstacles**) and this kept his performance in the moment, alive, real and full of depth. Instead of moaning about a long run, coasting and riding on the laurels of his already well established success, he instead transcended a long-term run without getting stale and continued to get high recognition for his in-depth and fully evolved performance.

I would encourage any performer about to embark in a long run to take a leaf out of this book and apply technique so every night will be fresh, enjoyable and alive.

THINGS TO AVOID WHILE REHEARSING

Never be tempted to rehearse in front of a mirror, this is not helpful at all to your development or characterization. The idea of watching yourself is not productive and can only promote self-consciousness; if acting is losing yourself in your character, then looking at yourself perform in front of a mirror goes against everything. So just don't. This also applies to recording your voice/lines and listening back to it; this is not a good way to rehearse and learn lines. However, using the iPhone/iPad app 'Notability', you can upload your script, write on it, highlight text and record the *other characters'* lines; this will allow you to rehearse alone and learn your lines and cues at home, in the car or wherever. It is an advance take on what I used to do as a student actor; I would tape-record the other person's lines and leave a silent gap for my lines. This totally enabled me to rehearse on the go anywhere, anytime. I have recommended this app to many professional actors and now they swear by it.

I once worked with a young girl who wanted to be an actor and was working very hard to get into drama school. She would come to me each week and I was getting increasingly dismayed when I did not see any improvement from week to week. She assured me she rehearsed at least an hour or two every night. Finally, after no progress whatsoever, I asked '*How* are you actually rehearsing?'. To my absolute horror, she told me she rehearsed silently. 'How so?', I enquired, as this was a new concept to me. She revealed she shared a relatively small flat with someone else and was embarrassed to rehearse out loud in case she was overheard; she therefore rehearsed silently in her head when she was doing the washing-up, and various other household chores. I have never come across anything like this before or since. It's the equivalent to a singer rehearsing their song silently in their head. Needless to say, this girl didn't get into drama school and this method should never be attempted. This takes internalizing onto a whole other level; never internalize feelings or emotions to the point that you are feeling it but nobody else can see it. Emotions and feelings must manifest not only internally but externally as well. I'm not suggesting that you over-magnify but what you're feeling mustn't be invisible even if you're in front of a camera, it has to be evident.

So you're in a play and your director tells you to go off and rehearse your scenes. This should not give you licence to direct your fellow actors or critique them. You can suggest to them and offer up your methodology but aside from that, it's not your place to direct. Again, try not to be tempted to rehearse and re-rehearse your scene. Try to work through the intentions. If your fellow actor has not worked in this way and you have the time and inclination you might want to help and guide them through some basic text break-down and focus on rehearsing with them; 'How are you going to make them feel, by doing what…?' By charming, scolding, threatening…? This is the most organic and constructive way to rehearse and I'm sure even if you don't reveal this to your director, they will see a vast improvement in your scene.

Never ask your director or teacher to give you a line reading and if you're on the receiving end of a teacher/director giving you one, take it with a pinch of salt. This is not a constructive way of directing; I'm sure you didn't go into acting to be a mimic or a puppet. Try to resist as much as possible following this way of working.

Never go on You Tube to watch scenes or clips of something you're about to rehearse or watch the famous film that was made of the play you're going to be in or study, unless, as I mentioned early on, English is your second language and you feel watching the film will help you understand the plot or the arc of the story – in this case only watch it once.

I was recently working with an actor/model on a monologue of a well-known play. Unbeknownst to me he found this monologue on You Tube and watched it several times. I couldn't understand why his monologue was so stuck and untruthful. He finally fessed up that every time he got to certain lines he heard this actor's rendition and couldn't do it any other way. Needless to say, we had to abandon the speech as his work on it had been unnecessarily tainted in the worst possible way! Lesson learnt, resist the temptation. Just don't!

Never act just on the line – you should always have an internal thought process going on in your head and I'm not talking about 'what's my next line'. When you're filming, the camera will most definitely pick up on the fact you're not in the moment if you are not actively thinking as the character. This is relevant for both film and theatre, you should act *in between* lines as well as *on* the line.

3RD EYE

This is the biggest curse for any actor. How to rid yourself of watching and listening to yourself? This can sometimes take actors a lifetime to achieve. If you're so self-aware or self-conscious that you're obsessing about 'how' to say the lines, then it sounds like your 3rd eye is definitely a problem.

You should not be watching, judging, critiquing or listening to yourself while acting. Your job as an actor is to get underneath the skin of the character and the only way you're going to be able to achieve that is to lose yourself in the character by being connected. Over-analyzing and over-thinking aren't going to help you get beneath your character. Initially you might have to tap into your head to understand the text but once you have deciphered what you need, you have to be able to turn off your head and allow an organic process to take over. Having a strong 3rd eye can be very destructive indeed. You may be trying to rehearse or perform and your 3rd eye not only watches what you're doing but also comments in the most negative fashion, telling you all sorts of things, like for instance how fake you sounded and that what you just did was crap etc. I'm sure you can all recognise this voice to a certain extent and maybe you'll never be able to totally rid yourself from it, however, you can work at lessening it considerably, so it doesn't end up destroying and hijacking you and your performance.

I have worked with many students/actors who have been majorly over-critical of their work. Having liked and believed what they did I asked them what percentage of their 3rd eye was present and they said about 5%. In honesty, I know this is going to sound like a complete contradiction but you should always have at least 10% of a 3rd eye present in everything you do. That way there will always be that small percentage checking in on your self-control and making sure, for example, that no characters get hurt if you have to hit them or have to react strongly.

I have indeed been around actors, in particular students, who thought the aim was to lose themselves 100% in their characters, otherwise this would mean they weren't real. This really is bullshit and I in no way encourage actors to be out of control and lose self-restraint, otherwise there will be accidents and incidents. I can happily say that this has never happened under my teaching or direction because I become that unruly actor's 3rd eye and stop the action immediately before any real damage is caused. I have known teachers and directors let improvisations and rehearsals get out of control, and in this one instance, allowing real knives to be used in fights and of course there will be (and indeed there were) casualties in such a foolish situation – an unbelievably stupid thing to do. Blood, stitches and hospital is not what true acting is about! This of course is crazy and if your teachers/directors don't have the backbone to stop something spinning out of control, you should at once do so yourself. Under no circumstances should anyone ever get hurt for the sake of 'art'. There should always be an element of control however real you want the performance to be. Know the limits. Submerge yourself consciously!

FILMING OUT OF SEQUENCE

This is very typical of any filming. The best way to stay on top of this is to make sure you refer back to your script and you know your previous circumstance and your state of being. A good preparation should help you get right into the zone, even if it's your first day of filming and they're starting with your death scene.

DISAGREEMENT

Ideally you should always be on the same page as your director. A good director should always talk to you about your character before and during rehearsals/shoot.

If you're in a situation where you've been left to your own devices to find your character and then you're on stage or in front of the camera and the director turns around to you and fundamentally disagrees with all your choices, you have to very quickly ascertain what they want or come to some kind of compromise. Often this can easily be resolved by making a few adjustments. This might be the time to trust and fall heavily back on your technique; by doing this you should be able to modify your character by altering your justifications and actions thereby giving the director what he/she wants.

What if you get involved in a play or project where the concept goes against your grain and you feel you would have to compromise your integrity too much? I guess that leaves you with two choices. You either suck it up and accept that you have to be in a production that you take issue with as well as accepting that you have to play the character in a way you don't agree with or you part company and quit. Hopefully the latter can be avoided if all this is ironed out in a conversation or several before you accept the job. It is perfectly normal for you to want to know how your director sees your character. If you really feel you can't see eye to eye with your director and his vision is the opposite of yours, sadly there's very little you can do, especially if you have a controlling director. You will have to make the decision as to whether you grin and bear it regardless or whether your disagreements go too deep and it's causing so many arguments and friction that finally there's no option but to leave and move onto a happier collaboration.

WHAT TO USE AND WHAT NOT USE, THAT IS THE QUESTION

Technique is there to help you, not hinder you. Don't forget, ultimately acting should be fun and spontaneous not a stressful, intellectual process. Some characters might come easier than others and that's OK too – acting really doesn't always have to be a struggle! You should not be aiming to try and use all aspects of the acting technique for every role and character you play.

Think of having a big acting toolbox at home and every time you have to approach a role you take the specific tools that you need for that part out of the box. You must understand that some characters will come easier to you and be more accessible than others. Great, lucky you! Others might be further away and harder to access and that's exactly when you should open your box and take out the exact tools you need to help you find the character.

9. FINDING DIFFERENT TRUTHS

I s there a difference between film acting and acting for the stage? Much less then people think. The biggest difference is the medium rather than the acting. It's the medium that you have to adjust to rather than adjusting your character. You still have to know 'Who am I?', 'Where am I?' etc. for both film and theatre. The only major difference is you don't have to over-articulate or project and you don't often play a transformational character on screen.

Theatre presents a heightened truthful reality and film a more intimate one. Often for screen you are cast to type therefore, most of the time, you are playing close to your own age and on your own physical centre. What you can't do is bring a theatrical truth to your character when you're in front of a camera, it just won't work. I don't mean there's one theatrical truth – there isn't and it's a big mistake if you think there is. For example, you may be cast in a Chekhov play and find that you can't bring a contemporary modern truth to this world or your character. You have to find the specific Chekhovian truth/world otherwise your style of acting won't fit or be believable in this play. I'm not talking about modern or updated versions of Chekhov – that's something different – although you would still have to adhere to that world regardless. You have to find this specific truth whether it's a Shakespeare, Brecht, Sam Shepard, Tennessee Williams or even Musical Theatre. You can't approach these genres in the same way; just because it's a theatre production, this doesn't mean you go into generic 'theatre acting'. Your research, approach and style should reflect the way you deal with text and character.

NATURALISM AND REALISM

Naturalism and Realism are the same acting style (just two different names) – a movement in European theatre during the 19th and 20th centuries that portrayed an illusion of reality as opposed to melodrama and used naturalistic stage sets. These terminologies come up in the same breath as Stanislavski and Chekhov.

I will differentiate the two terminologies by using the term **Naturalism** as a style of acting that we usually see on TV in the form of soap opera i.e. television/naturalistic acting. It's acting that mirrors real life, which is naturalistic, meaning these are recognisable characters; the publican, housewife, shopkeeper, school girl, office worker, nurse etc. This style is a reflection of everyday life – warts and all. You also have the wonderful Mike Leigh who uses this style to great effect in his films.

I will use **Realism** here to define a *heightened reality* style of acting, which is what you need for acting in theatre, whether it's musical theatre, Ibsen, Neil Simon or John Osborne. This is an acting style which is real and truthful but heightened at the same time because it's on stage. If it wasn't heightened you might not be able to hear the actors and if it was too *naturalistic* this might be considered filmic or TV acting. Therefore Realism is having a truthfully connected character that exists in a heightened reality world due to the medium of the stage.

The key here is understanding the difference between these two styles and applying them accordingly. The problems occur when you have an actor acting in a very 'heightened reality' way in film and conversely actors acting very 'naturalistically' on stage.

If you have only worked in film it's more difficult to transition into theatre. It's definitely harder to crank your performance up for stage than it is to do less for film. Theatre is a much harder medium as it involves more skills i.e. having a trained voice and body, whereas for film, as I've mentioned before, you are often cast to type so there isn't much transformational acting required.

Why is it you see so many (particularly) Hollywood actors play themselves? This is because they are known for their charismatic personalities and even if their early careers consisted of playing a variety of characters they later got typecast mainly due to the expectation of their audience – anything different would disappoint. So often a film's success depends on whether audiences like that particular actor and whether they will go and see the film that their favourite actor is in.

FILM ACTING

There are many pitfalls to film acting. Most actors, especially the inexperienced and theatre actors, fear overacting, doing too much. This is a founded fear as the camera picks up everything, especially on a close up. However, some inexperienced actors take their concerns too far and end up deadpanning their expressions, under-voicing and flat-lining/underplaying, in the hope they will be truthful.

Even though theatre is more skills-based, in film acting, you have to be even more connected to your character and have strong clear intentions. We should be able to see (not in an obvious way) what you are thinking and feeling with subtext. You often don't have a rehearsal period for film, so all the work should be in place prior to the shoot and ready to go by the time the camera starts to roll. In truth, you must be 'on it', connected to your character, have clear objectives, psychological intentions, hit your marks and know when it's a close up, wide shot or master shot. Without stating the obvious, for film acting you don't need to over-articulate, over-project, over-physicalise, over-emote. You just have to 'be' your character, in the moment, with clear inner thoughts and specific outer objectives.

TEMPTATIONS TO AVOID PLAYING

- Character and Characteristics
- Relationships
- Conditions: Physical
- Reactions and Attitudes
- Obstacles and Problems
- Emotions and Feelings
- Previous Circumstances
- Sense Memories, Affective Emotional and Emotional Memories
- Time Stress
- Animal Essence
- Ideas, Thinking and Decisions
- Personal Comments

What do you play if you can't play all the above...?
In short –

OBJECTIVES!!!

Character and Characteristics – Have them but we shouldn't see you 'playing' your character, you should just 'be' your character.

Relationships – We shouldn't see you 'playing' the relationship. There's a difference between trusting and just letting the relationship exist as opposed to showing us and playing the obvious.

Conditions: Physical – Hot, cold, tired, drunk, hungry etc. Have the specific condition you need but don't 'play' up to it, i.e. overly shivering or fanning yourself constantly. Just allow the condition to affect you accordingly without demonstrating.

Reactions and Attitudes – These should not take over. You should have them and then allow them to just be there and affect your relationships accordingly.

Obstacles and Problems – Have them but don't 'play' them and allow them to take over. They should be there and condition what you do.

Emotions and Feelings – Love, hate, anger, disgust, sadness, happiness etc. Don't indicate your feelings – just have them.

Previous Circumstances – This is for you to know and then you should let it inform how you make your entrance.

Sense Memory, Affective Memory and Emotional Memory – This is homework and we should only see the manifestation of the memory and not the memory itself.

Time Stress – If you allow time stress to take over it will ruin your moment in the scene. It should be 'immediate' but not urgent, there's a big difference.

Animal Essence – We shouldn't see the animal you have based your character on.

Ideas, Thinking and Decisions – We shouldn't see the character demonstrating or indicating they're thinking, having ideas or making decisions. Have an idea or thought and then respond – don't show us.

Personal Comments – You should never comment on your character. If you are playing an 'evil' or 'bossy' character we shouldn't see that 'you' think you're evil or 'bossy' (you should fully justify your actions) – that's for the audience to think or decide.

Relaxation

+

Concentration

+

Involvement

+

Belief

+

Truth

+

Feelings

which are sent into

Actions

which are

Objectives!

FINAL CURTAIN

Join the dots; if you were a singer you wouldn't dream of going on stage to sing an aria without training over many, many, years practising scales. The same for a dancer, you couldn't dance *Swan Lake* if you hadn't been training for years and years doing daily bar work. Why would you think that as an actor you can go on stage or in front of a camera and not put in your years of grafting, training and development throughout your career. Singers and dancers are training their vocal and physical muscles and this is no different for actors – your voice, body and mind are muscles that have to be continually exercised and kept limber.

Whether it's theatre, musical theatre, singing, film, dance, opera, ballet, mime or clowning – whatever medium you go into – there's *acting* involved and I believe it's not good enough to just go on stage or in front of the camera and just dance wonderfully or sing note perfect. One can often be left cold from a technically perfect performer if there's nothing behind it. That's called having a connection – you have to be connected to your material and attempt to have a fleshed-out character. Have a purpose – an objective. I can assure you, this will transform and deepen your level of performance.

I have noticed this particularly in Musical Theatre, Opera and Ballet and often get the feeling that the essential work of knowing who your character is simply isn't applied and there's a sole focus on singing and dancing – yes, to a high standard but empty of any true connected feelings, therefore coming across as very superficial and external. This can be remedied as long as you realise that you have to take ownership of your character and not settle for just singing or dancing beautifully – ultimately this is boring. I know I'm being harsh but this is the truth and it's about time there's an understanding that these skills are not a separate entity to acting and you have a responsibility as artists in whatever medium to be honest and truthful with the character you're portraying. It's a lot more rewarding to play and it's hugely rewarding to watch. Audiences are not stupid. They might accept second-best but if you show them the real deal they will be able to recognise the difference.

I have worked in all areas of the profession and with artists in all mediums. I really have the utmost respect for the actor who is that adaptable gypsy who constantly wants to improve their craft and better themselves and not just rely on their natural talent. A true artist and performer should be growing, developing and striving to be the best they possibly can. I don't deny there's hard work involved but I'm sure you didn't enter into the profession to wing it and sit on your laurels. Put in the hours, understand that it's your responsibility to bridge the imaginative gap between you and the character. Excel and strive – know and perfect your craft, make your own luck and reap the rewards, ultimately acting should be fun!

It's time we stopped compartmentalising the different skills and realising that it is yourself, 'the artist', you should be training. Keep it real, keep it focused. If you want to be at the top of your game, never take your eye off the ball and remember it's hard work, self-belief, confidence and commitment that will get you where you want to be. There is no reason why you can't be the architect of your own career!

I think it is fitting to give the master himself, Konstantin Stanislavski, the last words. Here are some of his quotes:

> 'In the creative process there is the father, the author of the play; the mother, the actor pregnant with the part; and the child, the role to be born.'

> 'What does it really mean to be truthful on stage? Does it mean that you conduct yourself as you do in ordinary life? Not at all. Truthfulness in those terms would be sheer triviality. There is the same difference between artistic and inartistic truth as exists between a painting and a photograph: the latter produces everything, the former only what is essential; to put the essential on canvas requires the talent of a painter.'

'Put life into the imagined circumstances and actions until you have completely satisfied your sense of truth.'

'If you know your character's thoughts, the proper vocal and bodily expressions will naturally follow.'

'When we are on stage, we are in the here and now.'

'One must not confuse the 'theatrical' with what is truly theatrical. The theatre undoubtedly demands something special that is not to be found in life. So the task is: to bring life to the stage, while avoiding the 'theatrical' (which destroys life) but at the same time respecting the nature of the stage itself.'

'There are no small parts. Only small actors.'

'Imagination creates things that can be or can happen.'

'Create your own method. Don't depend slavishly on mine. Make up something that will work for you! But keep breaking traditions, I beg you.'

And finally

'Love the art in yourself, not yourself in the art'

APPENDIX

(i) TRANSITIVE/ACTIVE VERBS

Accept	Berate	Change the	Convert
Accost	Bewilder	subject	Convince
Accuse	Bitch	Charm	Convict
Adjust	Blabber	Chastise	Coo
Admire	Blackmail	Chat	Correct
Admonish	Blame	Check	Corroborate
Adore	Block	Cheer	Corrupt
Advise	Blossom	Cheer up	Cover
Aggravate	Bluff	Chew	Cower
Ambush	Boast	Chide	Crack
Amuse	Bombard	Clarify	Cramp
Annihilate	Bond	Close the door	Criticize
Announce	Boost	Cloud	Cross-examine
Annoy	Bother	Coax	Crowd
Antagonize	Brag	Come on to	Crucify
Anticipate	Break	Comfort	Crush
Apologize	Break down	Command	Cultivate
Appease	Bribe	Commiserate	Curse
Argue	Bring to Light	Compete	Cut
Assault	Browbeat	Complain	Cut down
Assert	Brush off	Compliment	Cut off
Assure	Bug	Comply	Dampen
Atone	Build	Con	Dance around
Attack	Bulldoze	Conceal	Dangle
Avenge	Bullshit	Concede	Dare
Avoid	Bully	Condemn	Daze
Axe	Bungle	Condescend	Deceive
Back pedal	Burden	Condone	Decide
Badger	Butcher	Confess	Declare love
Bait	Butter up	Confide in	Decline
Bare your soul	Cajole	Confirm	Deconstruct
Bargain	Call their bluff	Confront	Decoy
Bash	Calm	Confuse	Deface
Batter	Caress	Congratulate	Defend
Beat	Cast a spell on	Conquer	Deflect
Befriend	Catch	Consider	Deflower
Beg	Celebrate	Console	Defy
Beguile	Censor	Contest	Degrade
Belittle	Challenge	Contradict	Deliver

Delve into
Demand
Demean
Demolish
Demoralize
Deny
Deprive
Deride
Describe
Dictate
Dig
Direct
Disagree
Disapprove
Disarm
Disbelieve
Discourage
Discover
Disintegrate
Dismiss
Disrupt
Distinguish
Divert
Doctor
Dodge
Dominate
Doubt
Douse
Downplay
Dramatize
Draw the line
Draw-out
Dream
Drill
Dump on
Ease
Echo
Eclipse
Edify
Educate
Elaborate
Elbow
Electrify

Elude
Emasculate
Embarrass
Embellish
Embrace
Empathize
Emphasize
Empower
Encourage
End
Endorse
Endow
Endure
Energise
Enforce
Enlighten
Ensnare
Entertain
Entice
Entrap
Envelop
Envision
Erase
Evade
Exaggerate
Examine
Excite
Exclaim
Excuse
Expose
Extol
Fabricate
Faint
Familiarise
Fan the flame
Fascinate
Father
Fatigue
Favour
Fawn over
Faze
Feign
indifference

Feign
innocence
Fiddle
Fight
Fish
Fix
Fixate
Flabbergast
Flatter
Flaunt
Flee
Flick
Flirt
Fluster
Focus
Fondle
Force
Forgive
Free
Freeze
Fret
Frighten
Fuel
Fuss over
Gamble
Gash
Generate
Get a grip
Get even
Get it straight
Gibe
Gird
Give an
example
Give directions
Give the facts
Give up
Glorify
Goad
Gossip
Grab
Grasp
Grate

Graze
Greet
Grill
Grind
Gripe
Grope
Ground
Grovel
Guess
Guide through
Guilt trip
Haggle
Hail
Halt
Hammer
Hamper
Handicap
Hassle
Heckle
Hesitate
Hex
Hide
Hinder
Hint
Hit
Hog
Hold
Hook
Hug
Humour
Hunt
Hush
Hustle
Hypnotize
Ice
Identify (with)
Idolize
Ignite
Ignore
Illicit
Illustrate
Imitate
Immortalize

Impair	their throat	Lust after	Nibble
Implore	Justify	Luxuriate	Nip
Imply	Kick	Madden	Nip in the bud
Impose	Kid	Maim	Nix
Impress	Kidnap	Make light of	Nudge
Incense	Kindle	Maltreat	Numb
Incite	Kiss	Mangle	Nurse
Incriminate	Kiss Ass	Manipulate	Nurture
Indulge	Knife	Marvel	Nuzzle
Infect	Knock	Mash	Obey
Inflame	Knock him/her	Mask	Object
Inflate (ego)	off his/her high	Massage	Obstruct
Ingratiate	horse	Match	Offend
Insist	Knot	Maul	Offer
Inspire	Knuckle under	Meddle	Ogle
Instil	Label	Mediate	Ooze
Instruct	Labour	Melt	Oppose
Insult	Lacerate	Mend	Opt out
Intervene	Lament	Meow	Orate
Intimidate	Lash out	Minimize	Orchestrate
Intoxicate	Lasso	Minister	Order
Introduce	Latch onto	Mirror	Oust
Intrude	Laugh at	Miss	Outdo
Invade	Launch	Mock	Outwit
Invalidate	Lay down the	Mold	Overpower
Invite	law	Monkey	Overwhelm
Irritate	Lead on	Mooch	Pacify
Jab	Lean on	Mother	Paint the
Jam	Lecture	Mourn	picture
Jeer	Leech	Mow down	Palm off
Jeopardise	Lend a hand	Muck up	Pamper
Jerk	Level	Muffle	Paralyse
Jest	Liberate	Murmur	Pardon
Jinx	Lick	Muscle	Parent
Joke	Lie	Muse	Parody
Jolt	Lift	Muzzle	Parrot
Josh	Lighten	Nag	Patronize
Jostle	Limit	Nail	Pave the way
Judge	Loath	Nauseate	Pawn
Juggle	Lurch	Needle	Peck at
Jumble	Lure	Negate	Peddle
Jump down	Lurk	Neglect	Peep

Persecute	Pressure	Razz	Ruin
Persuade	Prick	Reason	Rule out
Pervert	Primp	Reassure	Ruminate
Pester	Probe	Rebuff	Sacrifice
Pet	Proclaim	Rebuke	Salivate
Philosophize	Prod	Recall	Sanction
Pick a fight	Profess	Reciprocate	Satirise
Pick at	Promise	Recite	Savour
Pick up	Promote	Recoil	Scandalize
Pierce	Propose	Recount	Scare
Pillow	Prove	Recover	Scoff at
Pimp	Provoke	Rectify	Scold
Pin	Pry	Referee	Scorn
Pinpoint	Pull	Reflect	Scrape
Pinch	Pulverise	Refuse	Scratch
Pity	Pummel	Refute	Scrub
Placate	Pump	Rein in	Seduce
Play	Punch	Reject	Seize
Play the	Punish	Rejoice	Sell
innocent	Purr	Relax	Sense
Plead	Push	Relish	Serve
Please	Push away	Remember	Set record
Pledge	Put down	Remind	straight
Plod	Put your foot	Reminisce	Shake
Pluck	down	Report	Shake off
Point out	Qualify	Reprimand	Shame
Poison	Quash	Request	Share
Poke	Quell	Retaliate	Sharpen
Police	Quench	Reveal	Shatter
Ponder	Quibble	Revere	Shield
Pontificate	Quiet	Revile	Shock
Pose	Quip	Rib	Show off
Pounce	Quiz	Ride	Shrink
Pound	Rail	Ridicule	Shun
Pout	Rally	Rile	Sidestep
Praise	Rant	Rip	Silence
Pray	Rap	Rob	Simplify
Preach	Rape	Rock	Sin
Predict	Ration	Root for	Sink
Prepare	Rationalize	Rub	Size up
Present	Rattle	Rub it in	Skulk
Press	Ravish	Ruffle	Slam

Slap	Startle	Tiptoe	Waver
Slash	Steam	Titillate	Weaken
Slobber	Stifle	Toil	
Smash	Sting	Tolerate	Weigh
Smear	Strangle	Top	
Smooth	Strike	Topple	Welcome
Smooth out	Stroke	Torment	
Smother	Strut	Tout	Whine
Snap	Study	Trap	
Snare	Stun	Treat	Whip
Snarl	Suck up	Tremble	
Sneer	Suffocate	Trick	Whip into
Snip	Suggest	Tug at	shape
Snoop	Sulk	Turn down	
Snub	Sum up	Tyrannize	Whisper
Snuggle	Support	Umpire	
Soar	Suppress	Undermine	Win
Sober up	Surprise	Understand	
Soften	Surrender	Undress	Wish
Soil	Swagger	Unify	
Soothe	Sweeten	Unite	Wonder
Sound off	Sympathize	Unsettle	
Spank	Take a stand	Unveil	Woo
Spar	Take care of	Uplift	
Speak up	Take in	Upset	Worm
Spell out	Tantalize	Upstage	
Spew	Tarnish	Urge	Worry
Spin	Taste	Utter	
Spin a yarn	Tattle	Vacillate	Worship
Spit on	Taunt	Validate	
Split	Teach	Veil	Wow
Spoil	Tease	Vent	
Sponge	Tell a secret	Vex	Wrench
Spoof	Tempt	Vibrate	
Spook	Test	Victimize	Wring
Spoon-feed	Test the water	Vindicate	
Sputter	Thank	Vow	Yank
Squash	Thaw	Waffle	
Squeeze	Think it through	Wager	Yearn
Squelch	Threaten	Waken	
Stab	Thrill	Wallow	Yield
Stalk	Throw away	Ward off	
Stare Off	Tickle	Warn	Zap
			Zing
			Zone out

(ii) CHARACTERISTICS (a few examples)

Active	Efficient	Macho	Resourceful
Aggressive	Egoistic	Manipulative	Romantic
Alert	Emotional	Maternal	Sadistic
Ambitious	Energetic	Melancholic	Scheming
Articulate	Envious	Mercurial	Secure
Artistic	Extrovert	Modest	Selfish
Assertive	Fragile	Mystical	Sensitive
Aware	Fearful	Naïve	Sensual
Bigoted	Generous	Negative	Sentimental
Bright	Gentle	Nervous	Simple
Careful	Genuine	Obsessive	Sincere
Caring	Good natured	Open	Stubborn
Charming	Honest	Optimistic	Talented
Cheerful	Humorous	Opinionated	Tenacious
Childish	Idealistic	Organized	Tolerant
Child-like	Imaginative	Paternal	Trusting
Cold	Infantile	Perceptive	Trustworthy
Compassionate	Inflexible	Petty	Truthful
Controlled	Irritable	Positive	Understanding
Creative	Introvert	Practical	Vain
Crude	Insecure	Prejudiced	Versatile
Curious	Insincere	Prissy	Vibrant
Daring	Intuitive	Protective	Vivacious
Depressive	Jealous	Pugnacious	Volatile
Dependent	Kind	Rational	Vulnerable
Devious	Lazy	Realistic	Warm
Direct	Lethargic	Reliable	Witty
Dogmatic	Loving	Religious	Zesty
Down to earth	Loyal	Repressed	

(iii) IN-DEPTH CHARACTER/SELF QUESTIONS

What do you have in your pockets?
What objects do you always carry?
What is your best physical feature?
What is your most dominant character trait?
What is your best physical mannerism?
What is your worst physical mannerism?
What don't you like about yourself?
What is your greatest fear?
What would make you tell a lie?
What words or phrases do you most overuse?
What is the trait in others that you dislike?
What makes you most depressed?
When and where were you happiest?
What are your strongest prejudices?
What is your greatest regret?
What is your idea of perfect happiness?
What talent would you most like to have?
Who or what is the greatest love of your life?
What is your greatest extravagance?
What would most improve the quality of your life?
Which living person do you most admire?
Which living person do you most despise?
What is your favourite piece of music?
What is your favourite painting?
What is your favourite book?
Who are your favourite writers?
What are you reading at the moment?
What is your favourite word?
What talent would you most like to have?
Which historical figure do you most identify with?
How would you like to be remembered?
What are your attitudes towards the important people in your life in the play?

Dee Cannon started her career as an actress. She trained for three years at Arts Educational drama school in London as well as with Uta Hagen in New York. Dee then went on to act in a plethora of theatre tours around the UK and formed her own company, where she acted and produced a handful of plays on the London fringe and was shortlisted for the London Fringe Awards.

Dee then went on to run a variety of Stanislavski-based workshops around London until she was invited to bring her teachings to RADA in 1993. She was Senior Acting Tutor at RADA for 17 years and directed over 20 productions there. Since then Dee has been invited to direct professionally and give masterclasses, often sponsored by the British Council, in countries such as Sweden, Israel, the Philippines, Bulgaria, Germany and the USA. She has earned her reputation as being the foremost Stanislavski acting coach in the UK working internationally with celebrities and beginners alike in all aspects of the profession – coaching on feature films, TV, theatre, musical theatre and pop videos. Her work has been documented in several TV programmes, including Channel 4's award-winning series *Faking It* and BBC's *Blue Peter*. Currently she splits her time between London and LA working as a freelance acting coach in theatre, film and TV.

Publishing in 2016

The Oberon Book of Modern Monologues for Women:
Teens to Thirties
Edited by Dee Cannon
9781783199396

The Oberon Book of Modern Monologues for Men:
Teens to Thirties
Edited by Dee Cannon
9781783199372

The Oberon Books monologue collections revamped by author of best-selling *In-Depth Acting*, Dee Cannon. A brand new workbook format with speeches for actors with a casting age of teens, twenties or thirties.

Monologues are an essential part of every actor's toolkit. Actors need them for drama school entry, training, showcases and when auditioning for roles in the industry. Following on from the bestselling first volume (2008) and second volume (2013) this book showcases selected monologues from some of the finest modern plays by some of today's leading contemporary playwrights. The monologues contain a diverse range of quirky and memorable characters that cross cultural and historical boundaries and are organised in age-specific groups: 'Teens', 'Twenties' and 'Thirties'.

New features:

- Introduction by Dee Cannon offers advice on how actors can work on their pieces
- Greater choice of monologues – 15 speeches for each age group
- Introduction page to each monologue includes key character features like exact age and ethnicity for convenience when scanning through for suitable material
- Workbook-style blank page next to each monologue so that actors can write in their notes

The Actor's Toolkit

Acting: Cut the Crap, Cue the Truth Natalie Burt
9781849434799

The Clown Manifesto
P. Nalle Laanela & Stacey Sacks
9781783191192

The Improv Book
Alison Goldie
9781783191802

Shakespeare's Advice to the Players Sir Peter Hall
9781783190096

Acting Shakespeare's Language
Andy Hinds
9781783190089

Dramatic Adventures in Rhetoric Giles Taylor &
Philip Wilson
9781849434911

Keith Bain: The Principles of Movement Michael Campbell
9781783191093

The Voiceover Book: Don't Eat Toast David Hodge &
Stephen Kemble
9781783190546

How to Do Accents / How to Do Standard English Accents Jan
Haydn Rowles & Edda Sharpe
9781840029574
/ 9781840029901

Learn, develop and thrive with these essential books for actors

WWW.OBERONBOOKS.COM